Why Projects Fail

and

How to Succeed

Ed,
To a great friend
and a man I admire.

Doug

i

Other books by Douglas Fain

The Phantom's Song

2040 American Exodus

Anarchist for Rent

Why Projects Fail
and
How to Succeed

Douglas Fain & Mark Hunt

Bergen Peak Publishing, Evergreen, Colorado

This book is based on the combined experiences of the authors and suggestions from several of their friends who also work in the field of project management. Mark and Doug have over fifty years combined experience as consultants in project management and many more years as professionals working on projects around the world.

Douglas Fain & Mark Hunt—*Why Projects Fail and How to Succeed*

Copyright 2019 Douglas Fain & Mark Hunt

All rights reserved.

Printed in the United States of America.

No part of this book may be used or reproduced in any manner whatsoever without written permission except for quotations in articles or reviews.

For information contact Bergen Peak Publishing
2964 Elk View Dr.
Evergreen, Colorado, 80439.

Cover and book design by Lorna Clubb

ISBN: 978-1-7923-0221-3
Bergen Peak Publishing, Evergreen, CO
First edition: February, 2019

This book is dedicated to the project managers and their teams who get up each morning and go to work in order to produce the things the world needs. We hope this book will make their jobs a little easier.

Acknowledgements

We would like to thank Len Hawkins, Don Gier, and Rick Rokosz for their professional reviews and substantive suggestions. Their experience in the field of project management was instrumental in covering this complex and interesting subject. Finally, we send a salute of appreciation to the artist, Lorna Clubb, for her work on the cover.

"Having a copy of MS Project makes you a project manager to the same extent that having a copy of MS Word makes you an author."

Frank Parth

Table of Contents

Charts and Figures

Introduction

The dim picture on my computer screen was that of a face I knew well. Mark and I had worked on many projects together over the years, and my appreciation for his professional skills had, in time, evolved into a close friendship as well. Both of us have spent most of our lives (well over fifty years between the two of us) working on projects or consulting on clients' projects that had gone awry. He had just received a call from yet another client with a problem; another project was in trouble. Most of our careers involved saving failing projects, but occasionally we have also had clients invite us in at the beginning of some very important project in which they had invested significant resources or reputation. On one such contract for the British government, I recall a Member of Parliament introducing Mark as one of the two best project managers in all of Europe. (Most people would have considered that a big compliment, but I think Mark was a bit perturbed at being rated second.) I don't know who that other project manager might be, but he/she must be very good at this business to be included in the same category as a professional such as Mark Hunt. His record of successes is long and envied by many.

Not long ago the two of us shared a beautiful afternoon on the patio of the famed Cyder House Inn in Shackleford, England. Their outstanding fish-and-chips and the wonderful cider were enjoyed as we discussed the idea of writing this book, a chronicle of the various costly, and easily avoidable, mistakes we continue to encounter as consultants in the field of project management. As usual, we criticized the various project management organizations that fatten their bank accounts selling rigid processes for managing projects, all the while missing many of the actual problems that exist in the "real world" of business (like the proper way to plan complex projects). We discussed the numerous "certified" project managers who continue to lead failed projects and the enormous cost of those failures. Those failures, we began to realize, were surprisingly similar on many of the projects we had been called to save, and that conversation led to the commitment to write this book. It would represent our combined experiences, as well as ideas from respected colleagues with whom we have worked over the years.

As we enjoyed our cider, my mind wandered back to my first project as a consultant in 1993. I remember quite clearly the angst in my mind as I stepped into the office of my new client. I knew I was a good manager, and I knew I had considerable experience in project management. I had spent many years working with the best in the business (companies like Martin Marietta Aerospace and consulting organizations like the Center for Systems Management and Strategy Bridge International), and I had managed my own projects quite well. Yet, how would I walk into a room of competent people and tell them how to manage a project they had already worked on for over two years? How could I analyze a complex project that quickly? Smart engineers had already spent months or years on these problem projects, and now I was to discern the problems in a few days? Then I recalled a comment by a fellow Martin Marietta manager. His comment was that "good managers ask the right questions and recognize the wrong answers." I had known combat early in my life, and it seemed all the guns were pointed at me this time. Later that evening, however, I walked back into my hotel room, threw my materials on the bed, and smiled broadly into the mirror. The problems were clear, and the solutions were as standard as the notes in my computer. Twenty-six years later the same problems still persist on many projects, and the same solutions are still as applicable today as they were when I began my consulting career. Even with all the certifications and all the

2

courses and training in this profession, the same mistakes persist. Have we learned nothing over all these years?

Today project managers have a plethora of tools to manage their projects. There are numerous computer programs to help us plan and manage more efficiently, and we have bookshelves burdened with texts on processes and procedures. Project management courses are constantly offered by government organizations, corporations, and universities. There are hundreds of thousands of "certified" project managers touting their credentials, and still the number of failed projects continues to grow. If you compare the numbers of overrun, late, failed projects from the past with those of today, I suspect the results would be discouraging. Perhaps we managed better with just a pencil. There is a recent joke on the internet about how we built such huge numbers of ships, planes, tanks, armament, even the Manhattan nuclear project during World War II, yet in the same time today the U.S. government could not produce a functioning healthcare *web-site* with a budget of $800 Million. Perhaps even more embarrassing was the fact that they had no idea it would fail until it was finally delivered for implementation. Their test program was obviously flawed. These failures are huge and remarkably expensive, ruining reputations of people and organizations alike. The mistakes are also embarrassing, or at least they should be! The message is quite clear; we are doing something wrong, and we cannot afford to continue these costly mistakes, and make no mistake about it, the mistakes are costly. We read far too often of some project that was delivered years late with cost overruns in the millions or even billions of dollars. The opportunity costs of such errors are substantial. As I said before, we simply cannot afford such mistakes any longer.

Several years ago I recall watching a group of upset parents on the evening news demonstrating in the streets about a grammar school that had been closed in their neighborhood. It brought to mind the airport in that same city that had cost overruns of over a billion dollars. I wondered if any of those young parents had managed to link those two events in some way. How many grammar schools could be maintained with a billion dollars? Society's needs are far too great to be wasting precious dollars on mismanaged projects. Obviously those parents couldn't connect the dots; they re-elected the same politicians who had mismanaged the failed airport project just outside their city.

What is needed today is a focus on the dynamics (and the economics) of executing projects *right the first time*. It would be illuminating to calculate the number of projects we all know that have been redone several times just to *get it right*. How much cheaper would it have been to simply *do it right the first time?* The savings would not only have been in dollars but also customer satisfaction and reputation as professionals. There is an old saying that "we don't have enough resources to do the work right the first time, but we seem to have plenty of resources to do it right the second time." And, I might add—a third time, a fourth time, etc. When I see so many project failures, I often wonder what senior management was doing while their projects were crashing all around them. As I once told a vice president of a rather large company who was criticizing one of his project managers, "Well, who hired him? Whose job was it to ensure that he succeed? Where does the *buck* stop in this organization? Who is ultimately responsible for the organization's success?" The criticisms stopped abruptly. While I often see failures at the project level, I also see failures in the senior levels of organizations that are not managed well. Bosses are not payed to "watch." They also have a responsibility to engage in the work and ensure their managers succeed. Do the project teams need more resources? Were the original requirements reasonable? Did the original schedule and budget match the requirements? You get the idea. If projects continue to fail in an organization, then someone in senior management is also failing. The economics of *Right-the-First-Time* is an integral part of the new concept of success in management. PMI, PRINCE2, and countless other institutions that were focused on project management have provided some worthwhile fundamentals, but now we need to make the next step in the continuous evolution in business management. We need to review and refine our processes and procedures. What we have been doing simply isn't working well enough. When 80% of projects fail, we are doing something wrong, and it is time to change.

It is only appropriate to mention that although many projects fail and make the news, there are also those that succeed quietly. We occasionally hear of their successes, but often we do not. What attention can the media generate with a success story? Certainly, there are many obstacles to project management. We have done a great deal of research on actual projects, both successful and failed, and we have talked with many project teams about the things that made their jobs difficult. Some are obvious:

- Funding issues
- Customer indecision and lack of understanding of the technology involved
- Excessive customer changes
- Changing technology
- Risks and business uncertainty
- Sheer complexity of many large projects
- Resource availability
- Global sourcing issues
- Poor planning by both project teams and their customers

These issues and others are very real, but it is the job of the project manager to understand them, anticipate them, and develop plans to accommodate them. As a former American president, Harry Truman, once said, "The buck stops here!" Ultimately the project manager is the person in charge of the success or the failure of any project, but it is management's responsibility to ensure the project manager and his/her team have the knowledge, resources, and tools to accomplish that success.

With this in mind, the purpose of this book will be to review some of the major reasons why projects have failed in the past with the hope that perhaps we can identify concrete lessons that will prompt us to manage our future projects more professionally and successfully.

Projects are divided into very discreet phases that require various tasks and management operations. When these are neglected, or performed out of sequence, success is highly unlikely. As consultants we continue to see important tasks that are omitted for numerous reasons—tasks that could have led to success instead of failure. We will lay out the basic rudiments of what each of these phases include in the second part of this book and make some suggestions that should help any project manager as he/she initiates his/her project. Hopefully this will provide a map for our readers as they begin new projects.

Projects – An Overview

"If you can't describe what you are doing as a process, you don't know what you are doing."

W. Edwards Deming

As we begin, it would be useful to point out something we discovered as we discussed our many years of consulting experience. We uncovered something that we have not seen in the general literature regarding project management. Most project management texts and consultants look at project management from a *product* orientation. This fits Doug's experiences very well. He generally worked on projects to build "things." These vary from large items such as a spacecraft, a high-speed rail project, or multi-billion dollar national cellular infrastructure projects to things as small as a revolutionary new washing machine. Products, in our experience, also include software systems or on some smaller projects merely software modules. Mark, on the other hand, has spent much of his career working on *business transformation programs*. In many cases, some of his business transformation *programs* have included *projects* that were required to produce items (such as software systems) that were necessary for the program. We will address both in this book.

In our careers we both can point to individual projects we've worked on that were in excess of $4 Billion. We have also worked on some as small as $50,000. Surprisingly, all of these progressed through the same set of steps and the same set of processes. Only the size and the degree of complexity changed.

7

Project Phases: The Key to Understanding any Project

Projects have very distinct phases that they progress through as part of their project life cycle. Understanding these is essential for any analysis of project performance. There are many ways of explaining and dividing these phases (or Process Groups per the PMBOK), but for our purposes, we prefer to use four:

1. Initializing

    - Defining the project objectives
    - Developing preliminary requirements
    - Establishing contractual relationships

2. Planning

    - Developing, finalizing, and baselining the project's requirements
    - Establishing the team to do the work
    - Identifying specific tasks to be accomplished via a WBS (Work Breakdown Structure)
    - Establishing the Responsibility/ Accountability Matrix (who does what)
    - Developing the schedule and critical path (including master schedule, intermediate level schedules, and detail schedules as needed.)
    - Determining resources, both human and others, needed to accomplish the work
    - Developing the project budget

- Determining the risks and opportunities inherent in the project
- Securing management/customer approval

3. Project Execution / Monitoring and Controlling

- Managing the work of the project
- Tracking technical, cost, and schedule performance
- Managing changes
- Managing deliverables
- Completing Acceptance testing
- Project handover and customer training as necessary

4. Project Closeout

- Holding in-house and customer post-project reviews
- Completing follow-up punch list / warranty items
- Invoicing the customer
- Payments to the subcontractors
- Managing reassignment of team members

The reason we emphasize the phases of a project is because in our 50+ years of consulting experience, we both agree that probably 80% or more of the failures we have seen occurred as a result of errors made in the first two phases listed above. Many will find that surprising, but we suspect most experienced project managers will agree. If you fail to establish and manage requirements efficiently; if you fail to assemble a great team; if you fail to plan your project correctly, you will most likely fail to deliver a workable project on time and on budget. This leads to my comment that most projects fail in the first two months of operation. The mistakes may not appear until later in the project life cycle, but it was an error at the beginning of the project that led to the project's demise.

"NASA lost its $125-million Mars Climate Orbiter because spacecraft engineers failed to convert from English to metric measurements when exchanging vital data before the craft was launched."   Source: http://articles.latimes.com/1999/oct/01/news/mn-17288

As mentioned earlier, there are certainly many external factors that create a challenging environment for any project. These are issues that all projects face. They can be substantial; they can also be managed within the project's risk analysis program. With this admonition, let's look at the details of how project failures occur and also how those failures can be avoided.

Common Reasons for Project Failures

"Success is not final; failure is not fatal: It is the courage to continue that counts."

Winston Churchill

The reasons for project failures often result from a complex set of mistakes that are inextricably intertwined and related. As Mark and I compared our views on failure priorities one evening, we found we could easily agree on the top three. We have worked or consulted on many different types of projects, and during our discussions I maintained that the number one cause of failures had to be poorly defined and mismanaged requirements, but then I have mainly worked on *product-based* projects that are heavily reliant on having well defined requirements from the start. On the other hand, as mentioned earlier Mark has managed several large business transformations (where technical requirements may not be required until later in the project life-cycle), and he felt planning was the major culprit. His point was that capturing requirements requires a stepwise decision process that is generally carried out during the definition phase of the transformation process. Every good book needs at least one formula, so here's one from my good friend (and project management expert/teacher) Rick Rokosz:

$$TBD = +\$$$

Simply stated, the more To-Be-Determined or To-Be-Decided items one has at the beginning of a project the more it will cost in time, money, resources, or most likely, all three. Technical requirements drive a project, and if they are not understood clearly, success is unlikely.

Regardless of order, I feel we agree on the first two reasons for project failures—Requirements and Planning. I don't think I've ever worked on a failed project that did not include deficiencies in one or both of these two factors.

For the majority of projects that do not succeed we can identify a list of mistakes that contributed to the failure, but some mistakes are certainly much more damaging than others. We've agreed that requirements and planning are the two major reasons for project failures. I'll add *Failure by Choice* to round out the top three.

Top three reasons for project failures:

1. **Requirements management**— missing, incomplete, poorly defined, and changes to the requirements that were excessive and not well managed (sometimes called *scope creep*). See the formula identified above.

2. **Poor planning**—Between us we have planned over $30 Billion in projects during our consulting careers. We have probably seen two initial schedules in all those years that we considered adequate. We have seen schedules that omitted entire phases of the project and others that failed to include all of the items needed to build the project's deliverables. We have seen many that did not link the predecessors and successors correctly, or perhaps worse still, plans that were built months earlier and never kept up to date. The list goes on-and-on. We can do much better in this area. What we find amazing is that management on most of the projects with bad plans were not even cognizant of their problem. If your schedule is wrong and your team is working to a bad plan, you have a major problem. (more about this later)

3. **Failure by Choice**—these are the failures that occur as a result of management efforts to win business at all costs. These are bids that are "priced to win," even when the bid price is

insufficient to complete the work. (the same applies to the schedule)

As stated above, the reasons for project failures are many and vary depending on the particular project, company, customer, and industry. Experience is your best guide in this situation. Our hope is that by presenting our views, derived from many years of consulting experience, we can help you recognize and remedy the most common causes of failures.

Let's take a more detailed look at our list of the major reasons for project failures:

Poorly Managed Requirements

"Clarity affords focus"

Thomas Leonard

The main focus of this book is how to prevent so many project failures. As we will repeat many times, organizations simply can no longer afford the excessive cost of these failures. Competition in the global economy will not permit the sloppy management that has become so prevalent in the past few decades. If you do not have time to read this entire book, concentrate on this chapter and the next. They address the two major reasons for failures on projects of any kind or size—*poorly managed requirements and poorly planned projects.*

Failures in managing requirements can occur on projects as large as a new aircraft, a new national cellular system, a high-speed rail system, a major web site, etc. or on a project as small as a new software accounting process in a bank. It really doesn't matter, most of them stumble over the same impediments. Some years ago I was giving a talk to a local civic group on management, and project management in particular. When I finished, the first question from the audience was to name the number one reason for project failures. I instantly replied that the answer to that question was easy—Requirements. A project with a good set of requirements and a sound change control system has a good chance for success. One without those ingredients is destined for failure.

Poor requirements lead to project failures, but we need to remember that those requirements flow from other causes that also need to be understood and managed carefully – like poor objectives or lack of stakeholder involvement. Note that these go hand-in-hand. You need the right stakeholders to develop proper objectives, and these objectives lead to the development of proper requirements.

It is absolutely important to understand, therefore, that requirements flow naturally from the process of defining the objectives of the project. These objectives reflect the purpose of the project and are generally developed by a subset of stakeholders who will lead in the project's initiation. There are several key issues that should be kept in mind regarding project objectives.

1. Objectives, like requirements, tend to change over time and are seldom documented well or subjected to any kind of change control process as happens with more detailed requirements. This can lead to devastating effects on a project. At the beginning of the project the objectives need to be established and baselined. As the objectives mature and change, the requirements derived from those objectives will also need revision, and these requirements are the lifeblood of any project. It is, therefore, essential to document objectives in a Project Objectives Document (POD) and manage them carefully. The initial version of this is generally included in the Project Charter. We recommend that you place them under some kind of configuration control, such as a Change Control Board (CCB) to ensure they are managed well.

2. It is fairly common for project objectives to be vague or unclear at the beginning of the project. This can occur for many reasons, but one of the most common is that the customer has not yet fully considered, in detail, just what the project should do. The president of a small bank might understand that she needs a new software system for her

bank, but the details of just what it will do may well be initially vague in her own mind.

3.   It may be that the appropriate stakeholders may not have participated in the process of defining the project's objectives and may not even be aware that the project is under consideration. This will most likely lead to changes that must be managed and communicated later.

4.   The objectives may not have been reviewed by the major stakeholders to ensure that everyone is in agreement regarding exactly what the project should accomplish. A common symptom of this error is frequent changes in project requirements.

Once the project's objectives are established, the process of developing the detailed requirements can begin. Perhaps our consultant's checklist is a good place to start your requirements analysis. It has served us well over a large number of assignments and many years of interesting work. I personally developed this checklist (Note: I was a pilot—we lived by checklists) for new employees in my company, colleagues at various work sites, college students in my classes at three universities, and for one particular General Manager on a very large project in Asia who asked for such a document to assist in managing his organization. These checklists are included as appendices at the end of this book. As professional consultants, when we walk into an assignment and know we will be assessing a large project that has failed, we immediately refer to our Consultant's Checklist for requirements management. This is one of the more worn sections in that checklist since requirements issues are prevalent on so many projects. If you review that checklist, I think you will find it helpful.

In 1994 the Standish Group surveyed over 8000 projects and found the primary reason for failures were:

(1) Lack of stakeholder input.
(2) Loss of control over changing requirements.

16

(3) Incomplete/misunderstood requirements.

The Standish Group, 1994, "Charting the Seas of Information Technology," Dennis, MA

In other words, requirements were the top reason for project failures. We feel certain the same is still true today for product-based and most service projects, based on our own experiences and anecdotal data from colleagues and literature. Our first assignment then, is to change this trend.

In our consulting practice, we have seen numerous projects fail when one or two key groups (stakeholders) were not included in the development of the project's requirements. We have seen this from airport construction work (Denver International Airport comes to mind; the building was built before the requirements for the baggage system were completed. When those requirements were finally submitted, the system would not fit inside the building.) to the development of a communication system where no one bothered to ask the local firemen what their particular requirements might be. (They wear heavy gloves inside a burning building and therefore have very specific requirements for dialing a communication handset.) Many years ago, the Swedish King's flagship the *Vasa* rolled over and sank in the bay on its first voyage due to poorly managed requirements. Also, how many military aircraft were eventually overloaded with changes and could barely fly as a result? (The B-66 comes to mind. I once watched one crash and burn while trying to get airborne in Spangdahlem, Germany. I was waiting to takeoff in my F-4 Phantom on that same runway. It was not a pretty sight.) One of the primary jobs of any project manager is to ensure the project's requirements are established and codified as soon as possible. If some stakeholders are not included, the risk is enormous that the project will be delayed, over budget, and possibly a complete failure. I once read an article about requirements that included the following:

17

- A $421,000 fax machine – US Air Force. Who developed those requirements?
- 26 pages of requirements for chocolate chip cookies – US Army

There are numerous examples like these. They make us smile now; they also lead to costly failures if not managed well. So, we begin the process of managing requirements.

STEP 1: In the formative stages of the project, develop a Project Charter with appropriate management to define the project as it is understood. Project charters were initially the result of many Project Managers (PMs) clambering for their bosses to get involved to a significant degree at the inception of their projects. An experienced PM recognizes that his/her boss is also the project champion. When the PM needs extra resources or priority for some test facility, it is important that the champion be aware of the details of the work. The Charter represents the opportunity to achieve that goal. If done properly, the boss will approach the PM with a charter that lists the following items:

- A general description of the purpose of the project. This includes a realistic concept of operations which is a key ingredient in the initial development of requirements for the project.
- Background information on the customer (company/organization, department, individuals)
- Project objectives and deliverables
- General assumptions known at that time
- A preliminary high level schedule
- Initial personnel requirements
- Initial resource requirements/constraints
- Preliminary risk assessment
- Dated signature blocks for Project Manager and Sponsor

The PM and his boss discuss the charter, sign it, and the PM is assigned to the project. Then he takes over the future Charter iterations as more information becomes available. That is how it should work; how does it work in reality? Most of the time the boss calls the PM to her office and assigns him to the project. The PM is then asked to sit with the customer and develop the original version of the Charter. Later the PM and the boss will review it together and sign the original version to demonstrate agreement on preliminary data. The benefit to this approach is that when the PM writes the first draft of the Charter, he gets to determine things like the preliminary schedule, resources, etc. (I like doing that myself—I tend to be more generous to the project team than some of my bosses.) The key is that from the outset, both the PM and his boss have a common understanding of just what this project is about and what it is expected to accomplish. Then, when the PM needs support, he has a knowledgeable champion who understands the work to be done. As Dickens warned us, we should fear ignorance. It is not the project's friend. As a note, when I ask my graduate students in project management what causes projects to fail, resources are almost always on that list. As noted here, senior management needs to understand the basics of what your project is all about and also what resources will be required. (As well as the risks you face, the schedule you are trying to meet, etc.) If the PM starts a project with only a vague idea of what will be required to do the work, he/she will manage a very difficult project. The Project Charter is the artifact that documents those issues up front—for both the PM and management. It also authorizes the team to start work.

STEP 2: With your team and customer(s) make a list of all stakeholders for the project. Include everyone who might have an interest in the project. You may be surprised to find that the finance department of your customer's organization is also one of your customers. Likewise, training, quality control, maintenance, and many other support organizations have an interest in how your project will develop. A fellow consultant once told me about a bank that changed its software with a long and difficult project. When it was finally completed, the bank switched to the new system over a weekend and promptly had to close for two days— no one had remembered to train the tellers how they should use the new system. Let me repeat how critical this may be. If one stakeholder is absent in the requirements process, that single absence can precipitate a significant project failure. I suspect there was no maintenance representative during the requirements development for the 1973 Pontiac LeMans. If there had been, perhaps the 8th spark plug could have been replaced without removing the entire engine from the car. (I'm guessing we'll have many more examples of poor requirements than can be listed before we begin the second printing of this book.)

STEP 3: Set a date for the Systems Requirements Review (SRR) and invite all of the stakeholders to attend. As noted earlier, they will also be the key speakers at that meeting. They will present their requirements for the project, and they will defend them. I once watched a great systems engineer stand to present the requirements that had been submitted for the SRR on his project. He was butchered publicly by the same people who had submitted them. They noted things that were missing and asked questions he could not answer. He looked very out of touch by the end of that terrible meeting. I made myself a note. Let those who own the requirements present them at the SRR. That assures two things: (1) you will get a much more complete set of requirements initially, and (2) the experts will be there to answer the questions that will invariably arise. Think about it. If you ask most engineers to send you a set of their requirements for your project, they are most likely extremely busy and will therefore get their people together for a cursory meeting. You may well get a 60% version. Now, what if those same engineers knew they would be the ones to stand on a podium before a room full of engineers and managers to explain *their* list of requirements for your project. Also, for those companies with strong project management cultures, you may well have vice presidents, directors, and perhaps even your company's senior engineer in the SRR audience watching you.

I know one company where the president is a regular in most of these meetings. Why? He is smart enough to know that the success of his major projects – and hence his company – is largely tied to developing a great set of requirements as quickly as possible. He is there to add credibility to the notion that successful requirements management leads to successful companies. (You never see a half-hearted requirements presentation at one of his SRRs.)

What kind of performance can we expect if the owners of the requirements will be the speakers at the SRR? Not 60% for sure. If they care about their careers, you can expect more like 150%. One last point, when the SRR is complete and the requirements are ready for baselining, be sure to get the proper signatures. You cannot run a change control board if you do not have a signed, baselined set of requirements from which to manage inevitable changes.

STEP 4: Establish a strong project Change Control Board (CCB) with members from all departments that will be involved in the project. (I assume most corporations will have an established corporate procedure in place for this purpose— though I have been surprised in the past to find some very large corporations did not.) I have heard managers brag that there will be no changes on their projects. Generally, I laugh at that. They obviously have not been in the business of managing projects very long. Changes can be good for projects. They can give us better technology, better products, cheaper ways to manufacture things, etc. They can also destroy a project, however, if the changes are not well managed. That is where the CCB becomes important on your project. This is the group that meets for one purpose — to manage changes to the requirements. They

21

evaluate changes that are suggested by both the customer (Class 1 change) and/or the contractor (Class 2 change). This meeting evaluates anticipated impacts of the changes to the project such as cost, schedule, and technical issues. But if it is a really proficient CCB, it also looks at things like risks and political impacts (your customers also have bosses and careers—just like you). Customer satisfaction is so important to everything we do; what impact will the change have on that? Earlier in my career I was fortunate to work for a company that understood project management extremely well. At Martin-Marietta Aerospace if one of the members of the CCB could not attend a meeting to discuss a change, the meeting was rescheduled. Missing the impact of a change from only one perspective could be an extremely risky or perhaps very costly mistake. As they said, you can miss a meeting with the president of the company, but you cannot miss a change board meeting.

What do you do if your customer does not understand his/her own requirements for the project? If that happens—and occasionally it does—you have a serious problem. Mark and I have both seen this on a number of large, complex projects. I suspect the reason for this could be a number of items. (1) The project is just so large and complex that complete definition is extremely difficult initially. You will just get smarter as the project progresses. (2) Funding cycles. On occasion there is a rush to get a project into the government funding cycle, and that requires initiating it without sufficient time to complete the requirements process. It allows the project to get initial approval and funding, but it invariably leads to numerous changes in requirements and, therefore, cost overruns and delayed completion dates. (3) Knowledge. There are projects that only a small group of contractors understand well enough to establish a fairly complete set of requirements. In this case the contractors will often develop the requirements in a study phase and those requirements will then be used by the customer in the bid process later. I have seen this used by several customers. They actually contract with several bidders to study the project objectives and build a set of requirements on which those same bidders will later compete. (4) Accountability. If the government gets the requirements wrong, the contractor can always be blamed later, and the contractor will never complain. The government controls extremely large budgets, so nothing will ever be done to embarrass a government customer. You protect that customer at all cost. If a major government contractor ever pointed out the mistakes of its government customers, it would be out of business in a very short time. I once had a friend who worked for a major aerospace company who made the mistake of writing an article that was critical of a certain military project. It was published, and he was fired by his aerospace contractor the next day. Discretion is, indeed, the better part of valor, or, as some say, "is that the hill you are willing to die on?"

One approach that is often used today to accommodate vague or unknown requirements is the AGILE process. It is often used on software development programs with success. When the AGILE process is used, the project manager has a very important job to ensure that the team works diligently to stay on track and on schedule. Without specific baselined requirements and schedule commitments, it is easy to extend both cost and schedule targets.

Requirements are often referred to as part of the "front-end" process. This is the initial stage of any project where plans and requirements are developed. You might think of this as the phase where what will be done and how it will be accomplished are established. One of the key issues that I have noted over the years is the on-going debate of how much funding should be allocated to this "front-end" process. As consultants we have had this question directed to us many times. NASA and INCOSE have both conducted studies in this area with amazingly consistent results. When plotting project cost overruns against the up-front investment ratio it seems clearly apparent that roughly 5%-10% of the project budget represents an adequate amount to establish requirements and effectively plan the work. In both studies the organizations that spent less time/resources in this phase tended to have much larger cost overruns.

When we talk of customers, perhaps it is wise to define just who comprises this mysterious group. All too often we technical people tend to think the customer is the lead technical person on the customer's staff. That is just the beginning. As stated before, I have many examples of projects where some small group of stakeholders were forgotten and their requirements missed. Maintenance folks, trainers, logistics personnel, etc. All of these are stakeholders in your project, and all of them have specific requirements that must be met. Sometimes it is a good idea to just sit with the team for a few minutes and ask these questions: (1) Who are our customers? (2) Who are *not* our customers? (3) What do our customers consider to be of value? (4) What do they consider *not* to be of value? (5) How do we know we are meeting the customers' needs? These are important questions in maintaining customer relations over a long professional career. Those who may have done some work in Strategic Planning will find these types of questions familiar. It is wise to understand the answers to these questions as we begin any project.

Let me make one last comment about changes—especially in requirements. It involves the relationship between knowledge and time. The sooner a change in requirements is understood, the cheaper the resolution will be. Far too many projects delay the change process for many reasons (communications delays, need for further analysis, coordination requirements, or perhaps, just plain reluctance to make a decision) and incur both schedule delays and increases in cost as a result. This is demonstrated on the chart on the next page.

Figure 2: Cost/Time Projection

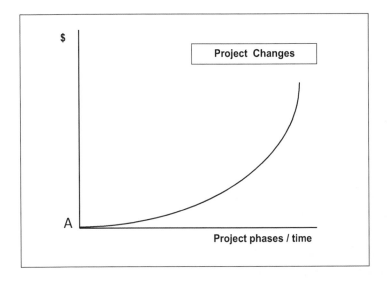

Perhaps one of the greatest risks we face on any fixed price contract is that when we bid it, we have, perhaps, our lowest understanding of the work to be done. We are essentially at point A on the chart, and the vendor assumes all those unknown risks. It can be a financially dangerous position for a company or organization to assume. The message on this chart should be obvious but is often missed, and that can be a very expensive mistake to make.

As the project proceeds, we get smarter about what the project is all about and how the work will proceed. Yet, when we estimate costs for the bid, we are most likely at a point of minimum knowledge about the actual work. This is one more reason that getting the requirements right and signed is so important. I have known companies that worked for years on a project with no established baseline for the requirements. You can do this in the case of a cost-plus contract, but I would not advise it. (You still have your professional reputation to consider.) On a fixed-price contract this is lunacy. It is a great way to lose a lot of money and fail completely. Sometimes we have a project we have done before (many times) and feel comfortable in our understanding of the work. That certainly reduces the risks involved. Still, I would advise getting requirements established, baselined, and signed as soon as possible, and, as was stated earlier, your System Requirements Review (SRR) is the place and time to do that. Everyone attends; everyone participates; and everyone signs the final set of requirements from the meeting. By the way, if your customer doesn't want to sign the Project Requirement Document (PRD), beware. There may be a reason he/she doesn't want them codified. I once observed a cellular operator who regularly got free cell sites by simply reducing the number of necessary cell sites in the Request for Proposal (RFP) that was sent to the infrastructure contractors, and later the operator added the sites back as changes. They had dealt with the infrastructure contractor long enough to know the new sites would most likely never be included in a change order charge. Essentially the customer (cellular operator) was purposely giving bad information in the RFP to their contractors and then getting the additional work free as a change. I recall angrily shouting at a vice president of that infrastructure company in a project review session regarding that situation. I also remember when that same contractor laid off over 50,000 people. Hmmmmm. I guess my shouts were not heard nor heeded.

So, where do the requirements come from? It is rather obvious that requirements are one of the most important factors for success on any project. If they are not complete, the risk on the project increases significantly. We have already discussed how important it is to get all of the stakeholders involved. We have also discussed the situation that occurs more often than one would expect—when the customer really doesn't have a good grasp of the specific requirements for his/her project. There is also the situation where all of the right people working together still miss key requirements. How can this be avoided? It is essential that the team be skilled at probing the stakeholders for not only expressed data but also tacit data that is not readily understood. This takes skill, patience, and time. The team needs to be particularly sensitive to needs, wants, and how requirements "flow down" to other requirements. Many companies use a process called a "Requirements Flow-Down Analysis" to ensure all pertinent requirements are identified and captured in the Project Requirements Document (PRD). Additionally, requirements can be elicited from interviews, focus groups, surveys, document reviews, etc. Another approach is the "what's missing" method. Don't look at what you have. Rather, step back and ask yourself, "What's missing? What did we overlook?"

Occasionally a discussion will come up regarding what is and what is not a legitimate requirement. I recall once seeing a PowerPoint slide asking the question, "Is it a requirement if it is not technically possible?" The answer to that question is really quite simple. I recall a boss I once worked for having a sign over the door as you departed his office. It said — "What does the contract *really* say?" The point is that the contract specifies the requirements. What you agree contractually determines what you must deliver. This brings us to a point of caution that is often missed. When you bid on a U.S. government contract, what you put in your proposal is seldom contractual. You can, for example state that you intend to get your spacecraft to Venus using anti-gravity. If you win the award, you simply win the right to negotiate the contract. It is at that point in contract negotiations that you will have to decide how you really intend to get to Venus, but you will not be held contractually liable if you do not use anti-gravity in your flight program. Most commercial contracts, however, will list the *order of contractual precedence* for the contract in the Request-For-Proposal (RFP). A commercial contract generally lists the following as related documents and incorporates them as part of the final contractual agreement:

      1.   The Contract

2.   The Bill of Materials
3.   The Statement of Work
4.   The Proposal

It is number four above that is often missed. On these commercial contracts you may be held contractually liable for things you include in your proposal. If you don't really intend to use anti-gravity to get your spacecraft to Venus, you most likely should not state such in a proposal if your customer is a commercial company. A note of caution: There have recently been reports of government agencies (both US and UK) that are accepting winning proposals as the initial contract baseline. The bottom line—read all contractual documents carefully.

One last comment about requirements. There is an area associated with requirements that can cause serious problems if not managed well. This is what we call Configuration Management (or Configuration Control). This is the process whereby we manage the configuration of the product we are producing. It has always been important, but the advent of large, complex software projects has only increased its importance. Having a clear and concise record of the configuration of our product is essential to managing any project.

As we progress with a project, it is important to have documentation that reflects what we are building and also the changes to the original specifications and drawings. Let me give you an example I witnessed on a project I had been asked to review several years ago. As I arrived, I watched several men loading equipment inside a large truck for a four-hour drive to a telecom site somewhere near St. Louis that had ceased operations. Their job was to replace several pieces of equipment at the site with the spares they were carrying. I was also there the next morning when they returned, very frustrated. They explained to several of us that the equipment they had taken on the trip was not the same as that which had failed; it was older and was not compatible with the other equipment at the site. The manager commented that it had been an expensive mistake with two men, eight hours driving, etc. I commented that he had missed the most important cost of all—he had an entire warehouse filled with old, outdated equipment, equipment that had to be scrapped at a cost that was actually in the millions of dollars.

There are so many examples of configuration management issues that they could comprise a chapter if we wanted. How many walls have been destroyed to repair a pipe that was not there at all? As you can imagine, this is critical for software projects. I worked for a client recently who had software teams from two different countries trying to repair a very important and quite expensive software platform. One team came from England and asked to see documentation that would indicate all of the changes the American team had made. (And there were many changes.) They had worked hard on the platform for months, but there was no documentation at all for what had been done. The last I heard, the customer finally stopped the hemorrhaging of funds and scrapped the entire project in favor of buying a completely new platform from another vendor, another mistake measured in the millions of dollars.

I was once asked how we could rather quickly discern the reason for a failure of a spacecraft that had failed in space. Actually, it is configuration control that allows such analysis. We know every piece of equipment on the spacecraft, its manufacture dates, the parts included, etc. We also have several of the same parts from the same batch, all of which have been tested repeatedly to achieve Class S status (Approved for space travel). We have documentation for everything on that craft. It was not touched without documentation.

Let me add one more item about Configuration Control. We've talked about the configuration of parts, designs, etc. The same is true for paperwork as well. Engineering drawings, technical documentation, schedules, budgets, contracts, and other important items (even units of measure) should also have their configuration controlled as well. One very public and embarrassing example is the Mars lander that crashed on Mars due to a major error on the customer's de-orbit calculations. The customer used kilometers but the spacecraft software de-orbit calculations were programmed in MILES!

Today most large corporations have Configuration Management departments. These are comprised of people who insure that this very important function is managed throughout the project lifecycle. In the case of smaller companies and smaller projects, this job typically falls to the project manager or someone he/she designates. Take it seriously, and do it well. The cost of failures in this area can be huge.

Planning: The Roadmap to Success

[Alice said] "Would you tell me, please, which way I ought to go from here?"
"That depends a good deal on where you want to get to," said the Cat.
"I don't know where. . ." said Alice.
"Then it doesn't matter which way you go," said the Cat.
                                   —*Alice in Wonderland* by Lewis Carroll

                          * * *

If you don't know where you are going, any road will get you there.

                                   Unknown

    The email started with a very specific statement: "You just saved us $12 Million." It had come from a vice president in a large telecom company and referred to a large international project that had been determined to be about three months behind schedule. At that point someone had wisely decided to call us for help. We have an excellent reputation for planning large projects and, since 1993, we have never lost a bid for a planning job. (With over $30 Billion in projects planned, that is a reputation for which we are very proud.) The vice president of that company and I both knew that we had saved him a lot of money (more than he expected) and that most likely we had saved his job, or at the very least, his position as a vice president in that company. (Losing $12 million is generally not a career enhancing situation in the private sector.) When I arrived in Australia and analyzed the project schedule, I determined that the schedule they had built was not worth the paper on which it had been printed. In fact, it was giving management erroneous information, and the project was further behind schedule than they realized. (The liquidated damages they were facing were actually nearly $14 million, not $12 million.) We threw away the erroneous Gantt chart they had been using and built a large network diagram (precedence diagram) with far more accuracy. Then, using a technique called *Walking the Wall*, I was able to pull the delivery date back to the needed contractual date. I knew the possibility of making the revised date was filled with risks, but the team was determined to make the project a success, and any amount of time they could save would relate to large dollar savings for the company. In the end, the project was three days late (not over three months as expected), and the customer said that was close enough and deleted all liquidated damages. As you might imagine, I immediately got a contract to plan a large number of future projects for that company. (It amounted to over $5 Billion in future projects for us to plan.)

After many years of consulting on projects in 31 different countries, I have made the following observations about planning.

- Very few companies plan well, and few understand the concept of project planning at all. Many even equate it with financial planning and budgeting which are quite different from planning the actual work required to complete a project.
- Many projects are late, costly, and customers are upset—leaving careers and reputations damaged.
- Professionals often don't know what a "good" plan looks like, and tools are misused or misunderstood.
- There is a misconception that planning is too expensive—just try running a project without one and you'll get a new perspective on out-of-control costs. Companies simply cannot afford poor planning. Professionals should know better.

- Bids are lost due to poor schedule performance. (Reputation is so important. I once was part of a bid scoring team for a major client. We were reviewing proposals that had been received when a vice president picked up one and threw it into the waste can nearby. When asked why he did that his reply was "That company is always late, and we cannot deal with late deliveries on this project.")
- Project recovery plans are missing or chaotic and therefore of limited use.
- Project status reports are of little value due to poor initial planning.
- Team members and subcontractors are frustrated with unrealistic delivery dates and inadequate planning.
- Earned value systems provide little value to many projects due to poor initial planning.

Very simply stated, planning is the key to managing a successful project. It is also the key to winning a successful project. Over the years I have planned projects for many proposals from avionics for the Aries I spacecraft to the Darfur project for the UN. A great plan is essential in winning new business.

When in doubt about the adequacy of your plans, our consultant's checklist contains a list of essential items which must be checked for any project. See templates in appendix.

One of the finest project planners who ever lived was a man named Earl Cook. He was often called a planner's planner. In my estimation he was the best. Most of what I know about this process, I learned from Earl many years ago. I recall him saying once that "the only time you need planning is when you are trying to get work or when you have work." Having a good schedule is essential in determining the cost and duration of a project, and those are essential parts of any bid. That prompts me to make a warning about bids. It is something I witnessed on several projects over the years of my consulting career. Never use a scheduling tool like MS Project to determine labor costs on a project. The reason is somewhat obvious if you think about it. It is a good move to load project resources into MS Project when building your schedule (it is a powerful tool for managing those resources), but never assume that will represent the cost of those resources. Your scheduling tool will total the cost of the resources needed to accomplish the tasks on your schedule, but what about the things that are done on a project that are not scheduled, for example, things like action item meetings, staff meetings, hallway discussions, etc. We pay people for 40 hours of work a week; however, we do not generally have everyone tasked on the schedule for exactly 40 hours a week—sometimes they may actually work 60 hours. What we kept seeing were projects that were on schedule but with huge budget overruns. A quick review of the project uncovered the problem—they had used MS Project to determine labor costs in their bid. Bad idea! This is a good time to relate another error I found on many projects that shared the same symptoms. What I also discovered were cases where the project team got together and built a Work Breakdown Structure (WBS) at the beginning of the project. They worked hard and developed a great WBS which was then delivered to the finance personnel. Then the planning staff and the engineers took that WBS and used it to build the project plan. That is when the changes became apparent. I recall once during a planning meeting when the team discovered they would need a test fixture. So, they added it into the schedule. Very good, except for one thing. No one notified the finance people that a new item had been added to the WBS. (Another configuration control oversight.) What that led to was a WBS and a project schedule that were not consistent. The result was a project that was scheduled well, but it included things that were not budgeted. The first time I saw this I was a bit surprised but added it to my consulting checklist. Since then we have seen it on several other occasions. It is a good idea to always have a communication avenue open between the engineers and the finance folks. I frequently find that to be missing.

Perhaps one of the biggest problems I keep running into regarding scheduling is the use of Gantt charts on large, complex, highly integrated projects. That is a mistake. A Gantt chart is fine for smaller, less complex projects, but on most large, complex projects you should use a network diagram (precedence diagram). Few people seem to use this great tool simply because they don't know how to build a network diagram with MS Project. It requires a little training and some software default adjustments, but it is well worth the effort. The major benefits of a network diagram are as follows:

1. It is very difficult for a team to identify all of the links (predecessors/successors) on a very large Gantt chart, and these links are key to the success of the project's schedule. I once built a Gantt chart for a client after several days of insistence that we should be using a network diagram. But my customer insisted on a Gantt chart, so I built one that contained over 8000 line-items. Finally, I was able to convince the client that we were most likely missing some key links. So I took a few days and built a network diagram with the same data base. When finished the team and I found almost 150 links that had been missed in our prior planning sessions. When I input those into the Gantt chart, it added over three and a half months to the duration of the project. That would have been a huge impact if it had not been caught in the planning process.

2. It is far easier to see and evaluate the critical path on a network diagram as compared to a Gantt chart. On an actual network diagram, the critical path is printed in red and is very easy to see and assess.

3.   One of the great advantages of a network diagram is that you can put it on a wall and get a dozen or so project team members around it at the same time to discuss schedule items. Gantt charts are very difficult for team reviews and analysis. Generally only one or two people can study the Gantt chart at any one time. Consider the project plan with over 8,000 tasks. How could a team of engineers study that together? With a network diagram, it is possible and remarkably efficient.

For those who are not familiar with a network diagram, I will add an example to demonstrate this technique. For large, complex, highly integrated projects we highly recommend this approach to planning. We have used this for years and have found it to be a much better tool than a Gantt chart for large, complex projects. This is a small portion of a much larger network diagram for a $450 Million cellular infrastructure project in the Los Angeles area. Each of the boxes in this schedule represents a task that must be completed. You can see that the "links" between the boxes demonstrate the precedence relationships of the tasks (with red on an actual diagram clearly representing the critical path). Additional information regarding each of the tasks is also included in the task box and can be changed to suit the needs of the project. It is a powerful tool when used correctly.

We have built network diagrams on major projects around the world and as team members on major proposals. On several occasions our clients have commented that one of the key ingredients in their successful proposals was the network diagram we created. Their customers found it impressive and commented on the significance of good planning on their projects. It is a tool seldom seen on most major projects today, unfortunately. Our goal in the Project Planning Academy is to change that in the future.

Figure 3: A Network Diagram

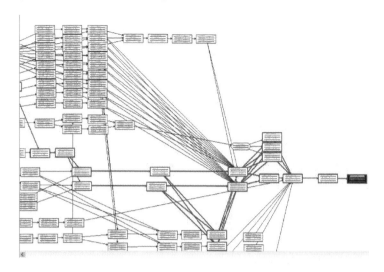

I mentioned the importance of adding resources to the schedule earlier. It is a very powerful tool in the daily management of a project. I recall a schedule that I built for a client in Michigan. I was staying at their corporate retreat near Lake Michigan one evening after everyone else had gone home for the night. I added a late input of a delayed prototype motor and was reviewing the resource loads when I noticed that the project would be short eight engineers in September. I alerted the project manager the next morning, and I recall his comment. "That's easy. This is May, I have lots of time to solve that problem, but if I had not discovered that fact until September, it would have most likely delayed the project three weeks." MS Project (or any one of a dozen or more similar tools) is simply a tool to give you data that will help you make better decisions. The resource loading function is one that will ensure you have the proper resources to accomplish the schedule you have developed. (One small note: I have seen situations where the resource graph actually showed too many resources during certain time periods on a schedule—much to the consternation of some team members.) By loading the resource data into the schedule, the team can compare resource requirements with the critical path and determine if there are non-critical elements (individual tasks) that can be delayed or stretched, thereby saving resources. The PM makes the decisions on a project— the tool is simply a way to get the information needed to make timely and appropriate decisions.

In our consulting business there is one other problem we consistently see regarding planning. Plans must be updated and kept current. I have seen decisions made with a schedule that had not been updated for over a month. That is asking for problems. Schedules change daily. Deliveries are made early or late, tests are failed and must be repeated, tasks are finished early or late depending on a myriad of items. These things must be noted and updated on the master project schedule. Today this is easy. You simply make the change, and it is reflected in the schedule posted on the project web site. You may decide to "reprint" the schedule as needed depending on the types of changes that occur, but the master schedule posted online must be updated. What I fear is something I have seen several times in my career. I once walked into a client's work area to help on a new project. As I walked down a hallway, I stopped to look at the progress on a schedule I had built for them on another project several months prior. It was still hanging where I put it, and it looked the same as the day I put it there—three months earlier. No one had maintained the network diagram; it was not current, yet they were using it to make important decisions on their project. Either the project was progressing exactly as I had planned it (highly unlikely), or they were using an outdated plan that was giving them bad information.

To summarize:

1. Build a great schedule to assure success. Start with your WBS. (You will need a professional planner to ensure it is done well. I have seen far too many mediocre plans lead to failures on important projects; there is no excuse for that type of management.) A quick thought. The WBS is the key for so many things on a project. It will be the starting point for your schedule. It will be the foundation for all of your financial reports. You simply have to get this right. Oddly, what I typically find is that most people really don't know how to build a WBS if they are simply handed a blank sheet of paper for a project that has just been won. For those working on large government projects, there are WBS templates in the Federal Acquisition Regulations (FARs) that you can tailor to fit your particular project. The reason the government decided to develop these templates is that on their cost-plus contracts, it is essential that the contractors' WBS and theirs be exactly alike. Since it will be the foundation for the financial reporting and management, they must be the same. But for those working on most commercial projects, you may well be handed a blank sheet of paper and asked to build a WBS. I find few professionals who really know how to do that. If in doubt, hire a professional or send your people to the right training program. Mark and I both recommend the Project Planning Academy to our clients.

(www.projectplanningacademy.com)

2. Planning is a team effort. It is not something that one or a few people can accomplish. You will need the expertise of the entire team, and you will get their commitment to the plan when they participate in building it. If you expect one or two planners to plan the entire project, your knowledge of project management is lacking. Planning is a team effort.

3. If your project is large, complex, and highly integrated, use a network diagram. A Gantt chart can be used for

presentation slides, but the project *Plan* should be a network diagram.

4. Always add resources to your plan. It takes very little time relative to the overall planning effort, and it is a valuable asset in managing your project.

5. Do not "level" the resources in your project plan unless you have the luxury of extending the end date of the project. *Level Loading* your project will invariably add time to your schedule. In all our years of consulting, we have never been asked to extend the completion date of a project. The issue is always the opposite—how to complete it as quickly and efficiently as possible. Just remember that if you level load your project it will solve your resource shortages, but it will invariably extend your end date. If that delay is not acceptable, there are several other ways to solve a resource shortage. Subcontractors, job shoppers, new hires, moving resources from other divisions, etc. can help solve the shortages while maintaining your schedule commitments.

6. Keep your plan up to date. An old plan will give you bad data. (Make the schedule "read only" on your server. No one "dinks" with the schedule except the project planner. Configuration control on the schedule is essential.)

A final thought for those of you who seek to become successful project managers. Pay close attention to this advice; it will make all the difference in your list of project successes. Find and hire the finest planner you can locate. The project planner is not the most skilled worker on your project, but he/she will have an inordinate influence on your project's success. Our Project Planning Academy trains and certifies project planners. They don't get that certification until we are entirely convinced they are professionals ready to handle any planning situation that may arise. How do you know if an applicant is a real professional in this field or not? One easy way to thin the list of applicants is to ask a few important questions such as those listed below:

1. Have you built a precedence diagram with MS Project or a similar tool in the past? How large was that project? Do you know how to create the critical path and manage it?
2. Do you use resource loading in your schedules?
3. Have you ever "leveled" a project plan?
4. How often have you built a WBS from scratch?
5. How often do you normally update your project plan? How do you baseline your schedule and maintain configuration control over it? Who is authorized to change the schedule?
6. What process do you use for updating a schedule? For re-baselining a schedule?
7. What is the largest number of nodes you have planned on a network diagram?

Schedule integration. This is a very important aspect of managing any schedule. In today's world of global business, we often see work being done across the globe and then integrated at one or two sites. Boeing's new Dreamliner aircraft is a great example of this. It was designed with collaboration from suppliers around the world. Final assembly is accomplished at two locations, the Boeing Everett Factory in Everett, Washington, and the Boeing South Carolina factory in North Charleston, South Carolina. Subcontracted assemblies for this plane come from many different companies around the world:

- Mitsubishi Heavy Industries, Japan,
- Alenia Aeronautica, Italy
- Korea Aerospace Industries, South Korea
- Global Aeronautica, Italy;
- Boeing, North Charleston, US;
- Kawasaki Heavy Industries, Japan;
- Spirit AeroSystems, Wichita, US;
- Korean Air, South Korea

- Latécoère, France
- Saab AB, Sweden
- HCL Enterprise India
- TAL Manufacturing Solutions Limited, India
- Labinal, France
- Korean Air, South Korea
- Messier-Bugatti-Dowty, UK/France
- Hamilton Sundstrand, Connecticut, US

Managing a diversified project of this scale is truly a challenge for even the best project management teams. This type of diversified work demands an equally diversified, but integrated, schedule. I recall a large government project that had work performed all over America and several different countries. I happened to be the planning manager on that $4.5 billion project. (The network diagram for that project contained over 20,000 nodes and was backed up by many layers of intermediate and detail schedules from numerous contractors and subcontractors.) Parts were coming from all over the world to Denver where they were then integrated into the final product assembly. In a case like that, it is absolutely essential that all parts are scheduled and then controlled to arrive at the right time to allow an efficient production schedule. One small part that is late can stop work across the entire project, and that can lead to a very expensive delay. It is imperative that all items on the schedule be integrated into the total planning process. It is also important that communication and control functions be timely and accurate. I once watched a director of a very large aerospace company demoted to manager in a status meeting when it became apparent that he had been less than truthful about the status of his organization's schedule progress. Everything on the schedule must work together. Honesty is essential for all of that to happen. Needless-to-say, the demotion of a senior director is a lesson that does not go unnoticed. Another great example of this involves using caution when dealing with large government contracts:

Your immediate government contact has a reporting chain that is different from that in your own company. Be sure to, as much as possible, ensure that the progress information you give to your company management is the same that is going up the government chain. I have seen very good program managers fired because the senior government customer was not being given timely or accurate project status – by his own people!

I would like to mention another schedule related error that I have seen as a consultant. It involves the bidding and awarding of a contract. The team builds a schedule as part of the bidding process, then they return to their normal jobs. Later it is announced that the company won the bid and many of those who worked on the proposal are selected to execute the contract. They all report for the new job with one huge mistake in their minds. They inherently think that the project they have won is the same as the one they bid. Generally, that is not the case. In many instances there are significant differences in what was initially proposed and what the final contract specifies. A great deal happens between the submission of a proposal and the awarding of a contract. Be aware, and do a very thorough job of analyzing the revised requirements specified in the new contract.

Before closing the discussion on scheduling, I'd like to cover a very important issue that almost became a chapter on its own. One of the major items that delays projects is late decisions—by either customer or contractor. This is a topic that is near and dear to my heart. I have railed against this for years. (with little success, unfortunately) When changes are needed on a project, if the team takes weeks to "think about it" before it is ever submitted for consideration and approval, or if a customer cannot decide if he/she really wants a red one instead of a green one, all those delays are expensive. Remember that not making a decision is, in effect, a decision in-and-of itself. I demonstrated the impact of the cost of changes over time in an earlier chart. (See figure 2 on page 25) Another way of looking at this same chart is to imagine a common decision made at different times in the life of the project. Notice on the chart below that the cost impact to the project is directly related to the time needed to make a decision. If a decision to implement a change is made during the design process, the cost and impact to the project are minimal. If that same decision is made during fabrication or during integration and testing, the cost eventually increases asymptotically.

Figure 4: Cost Impact Chart

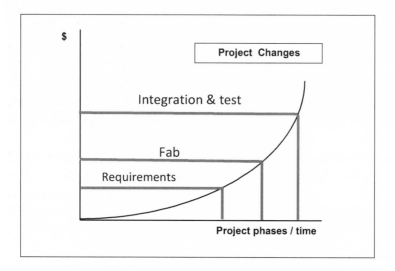

I became so concerned about decisions on a particular project early in my career that I dug through my old OR (Operations Research) books and developed a computerized tool to help my less confident colleagues with their decision making process. I was working on a project in China years later and one of the engineers there suggested that he had a good tool for making decisions. It was mine. I have to say it made me smile. I've been giving that tool to clients, students, and friends for many years. I guess it has traversed the globe now. Join my crusade, let's have well thought out decisions and let's endeavor to have them decided expeditiously. (If you send a note to

<u>doug@cebgconsulting.com</u> and refer to this book, I'll be glad to send you a "soft" copy of this tool.)

Project planning is a complicated and extremely important part of any project. It plays a major role in the success or failure of the project, the customer, and the company/team that is implementing the project. It is one of the major issues both Mark and I look for when we are called to help save a failed project. As mentioned, the Project Planning Academy has a comprehensive set of planning courses as well as their certification program. I shall certainly not try to cover all of that material here. It begins with the task of planning a major project correctly; then it covers the techniques of using the plan to manage a complex project by incorporating changes and unexpected events. Finally it goes into the magic of how to best shorten a project that is late and at risk of a major schedule failure. I will close this with a quote I often use by Sir John Harvey Jones:

"Planning is an unnatural process; it is much more fun to do something. And the nicest thing about not planning is that failure comes as a complete surprise rather than being preceded by a period of worry and depression."

Failure by Choice

"Failure is simply the opportunity to begin again, this time more intelligently."

Henry Ford

As we looked at failed projects over the course of our careers, Mark and I realized that there was one type of failure that we both saw on many occasions that is seldom addressed in project management literature. We have seen this situation in the past, but not to the degree that it seems to be occurring now, and it is disastrous for any project. I will note that this is not the greatest source of project failures, but it is growing quickly, and it occurs before the project even begins. We have given this situation the name "failure by choice," but another name often used when an external customer is involved is "buying the contract." Let me explain the type of failure to which I am referring. For years we have seen the following situation plaguing projects of all kinds and sizes. On a few occasions we became so incensed that we debated with our customers at great length about such a common, but dangerous practice. Let me give a hypothetical example. The salesman for company A sells a project for $20 Million and a schedule promise date of one year when in actuality the "real" cost to complete the work will be over $35 Million and the "real" schedule to complete the job is two years. A project manager and his/her team are then assigned the project, and they do an excellent job, completing the work for $30 Million ($5 Million savings from the actual cost) and in 18 months (a six month schedule saving compared to a reasonable schedule) What is the result? The salesman gets a large bonus and a trip to Hawaii with his/her family. The PM and his/her team are considered a failure since the project overran both its original *contract* budget and *contract* schedule (both of which were unrealistic). Unfortunately, this happens far more often than you might imagine.

In some industries the bidding competition is so intense that senior management and sales departments are forced to take extreme risks in their proposals simply to be competitive and win contracts. We once had a meeting with some senior executives in a large telecom company regarding this process. Their sales force was slowly killing their company, and their project teams were totally demoralized. The sales folks were selling large, very expensive telecom projects by offering schedules and prices that were simply inadequate to do the job. They were making promises that were impossible to meet. We suggested that perhaps the company should look at their incentive compensation system. They were incentivizing their sales people to sell projects, not make a profit for the company. There is a difference in these two goals. I suspect I could sell every car Ford could produce in a year if I get to determine the price at which I sell them. If you lower the price enough, you can sell most anything, while driving your company into bankruptcy at the same time. Perhaps a better idea would be to incentivize the sales team *and* the project team together. If the project makes a profit, they both get bonuses. If it loses money, then there are no bonuses for either. What this would accomplish is to incentivize the sales people and the project team to work together. We felt that particular company would benefit greatly if the sales people used the project staff more effectively in the bid process. (After all, it is the project team that best understands the actual cost and schedule associated with building a large cellular system.) Likewise, we felt the technical people building the system could benefit greatly by including sales personnel in their dealings with the customer during construction. (Who better understands the customer in that particular industry?) By working together, the sales force and the project team would surely strengthen both sides of that equation, and the company could become more profitable. In today's business lingo, this is a Win-Win situation.

A few years ago, I was discussing the subject of failed projects with one of the most accomplished men I know in the field, Len Hawkins. Len has climbed many rungs on the tall ladder of his success. By the time he achieved the position of Vice President of Engineering at BAE, he had scrutinized most every aspect of project management in detail. As we sat in his kitchen discussing failed projects we both arrived at this same conclusion. Many failed projects are simply perceived as failures due to the fact that the original bids were destined to lead to failure. In today's highly competitive world of large contracts the bidding is intense. If one analyzes the profit levels included in most government proposals, for example, they are amazingly low. (I am thinking of aerospace and related defense industry contracts at this time.) To win bids (i.e., survive) in a "lowest bidder" environment, every company must play the game. In order to win contracts, you must submit bids with overly optimistic schedules and completely unrealistic prices to be considered competitive. You then justify your bid to your own management and the customer by declaring a technological breakthrough or a "robust risk management program," or some other euphemism for "I'm bidding what I have to in order to win the contract!" If you bid what you and your team consider to be *actual* costs and schedules, you will lose the bid and soon be out of business. The customers know the bids are not real; the contractors know they are not real; and everyone hopes for enough changes in the system to pass the breakeven point with sufficient profit to stay in operation. It is a tough business, and the bidding and evaluation process has changed somewhat by emphasizing the lowest *credible* bid, but the process still needs to be led by strong, ethical customers who demand reality in the bidding process. However, when personal success is facilitated by weak or inexperienced customers and/or a faulty bidding process, the incentives usually drive bidders toward risky and unrealistic schedules and pricing. Unfortunately there seems little incentive to change.

A few years ago, I witnessed a bidding situation where five of the best companies in a particular industry all submitted bids between $23 Million and $28 Million for the same item. A sixth company entered a bid of $9 Million. It was completely out of range of normal costs for doing that kind of work. It had to be a joke, right? Guess who won. Could the work be done at that price? Definitely not. It was what is often referred to as *buying business*. As one old engineer stated, "The only thing worse than losing a bid is winning without enough money to do the work." Perhaps there was a strategic reason that company had to win that particular contract. Nevertheless, I suspect it ended up on some third page news report touting how poorly another government project had been managed. The contractor and the government agency were both probably embarrassed, but the process continues. (Where is senior management in all of this?)

We have seen the prior mistake played out over many industries and organizations. It effectively ensures failure on so many levels. Customers and contractors alike need to acknowledge this mistake and find ways to stop its occurrence. Another point. It should be noted that we hold many customers responsible for some of these poor business practices. Contractors will do what is necessary to win business and continue operations, but a strong customer can do much to put reality back into the bid process on large government projects. A bid that is obviously too low should be tossed immediately. (This is where the concept of *credible* comes into play.) Awarding an obviously low bid sends a message to the industry and to the general public that further erodes confidence in the free market and government institutions. Projects awarded on price alone generally end up as just another negative headline alluding to incompetence in production, management, etc., another government project late and grossly overrunning its budget. If a customer needs to "spread the wealth" a bit, that is fine, but do so with a "sole source" contract. The other companies don't need practice writing proposals, and the public is quickly tiring of large, failed government contracts. Truth is a powerful tool when used consistently. One last point for government contracts: Although it is often felt that governments have infinite funds for various programs, the US and especially the UK defense budgets are limited, given the demands placed on them. It is pretty much a zero-sum game; budget overruns on one program usually impact funding for other programs, often causing unexpected and unplanned changes—even cancellations.

The above conditions are not limited to aerospace and defense. I am sadly aware of a particular telecom company that lost millions in a similar situation. While the aerospace company in the first example probably knew their bid was below cost, I'm fairly sure the telecom company was not fully cognizant of the degree to which they had trimmed their profit margins. They exacerbated the situation by performing most any change order the customer wanted without charge, literally free change orders throughout most of the project. A smart customer will soon discover how to use that to their advantage at bidding time. If you need 100 cell sites, you simply put 85 in the RFP and later get the others free as a change order. This is particularly easy if the contractor is habitually late and apologetic for poor schedule performance. When will they ever learn the truth about proper planning?

I briefly alluded to the demoralized team that had worked so hard on a project, only to see it fail. Perhaps their only fault was that they accepted the assignment in the first place. It would have been smart to simply ask to be assigned to another more reasonable project with at least some chance of success. One of our clients, John Powers, who was an experienced project manager in the telecommunications field did this and refused to accept a project some years ago. I felt certain he would be fired for his argumentative tone with a senior vice president in his firm. I recall him shouting, "I refuse to fail because you don't understand the work!" He went on to tell the VP to find another PM who was inexperienced or dumb enough to take the impossible project. "After he fails, call me, and I'll fix it." That is exactly what happened. When the company realized it was about to lose several million dollars in liquidated damages, the VP called the original experienced PM and told him he could have whatever resources he needed to complete the project. I will note that this particular PM went on to become the president of a major telecom company later in his career. John's record of successful projects is well known by everyone in the industry, and his successful career is evidence that the admiration of his peers is well founded.

I understand that some projects *must* be won for various strategic reasons. Losing money is acceptable, if necessary, to win such strategic work. There are ways, however, to accomplish this without destroying project teams. One of our clients has an unusual approach for such "must win" projects. In that company, the PM and the team are assigned the project with the notation that it is *not* an *80-20* project. What does that mean? It means that the project does not meet the normal criteria of at least an 80% chance of success. Once the boss and the PM reach such an agreement it means that if the project is late and over the assigned budget, it will not be a negative mark against the team. It also means that if the project is somehow successful, then the PM and his/her team are heroes and will be rewarded very well. Frankly, this is not just a project management issue—it is a *management* issue.

Other Common Mistakes that Lead to Failures

As mentioned earlier, there are many reasons that lead to failure of projects. Often they work in concert; on rare occasions they work singularly. We have agreed that the top three listed earlier (Requirements, Planning, and Failure by Choice) are major culprits in the battle for successful projects, but those listed on the following pages are also challenges that must be managed in order to succeed in this important business. While the remaining issues are not listed in any specific order, they are all important. Read and heed.

The Project was not Required in the First Place.

"It's not worth completing that which shouldn't have been started in the first place."

Peter Turla

I know this seems obvious, but one must "Validate the Project." When working on an internal project (as opposed to a project contracted with an external customer or client), it is essential to understand where it fits within the strategic business plan of the organization. Don't assume this is understood just because you have been asked to initiate the project; it is part of the project manager's job to ensure that the project has a reasonable chance of success. If it were created on a whim, many hours of effort trying to win the hearts and minds of senior people to sponsor the project may have been wasted, and it will most likely be cancelled before it even starts. If it does rise to the level of initiation, it may well waste resources and time that could have been used on far better opportunities. These opportunity costs are real and very expensive for organizations. Both senior management and project managers have the responsibility to ensure that these projects are identified, evaluated, and cancelled. This is especially true for software or business systems changes.

Map the project to the business and operational objectives that it supports, then define how the business objectives support the organization's vision and mission. If this is not possible, then the reason for starting the project should be challenged. There have been instances where we have worked with executives to map projects to business objectives that have resulted in several projects being cancelled as the link simply could not be established. This saved time and money and freed resources to be deployed on projects that were a priority. This process provides validation of the project and also the business and operational context in which the project was conceived.

It is frustrating when a project you may have spent a lot of time and effort on is cancelled because it was never really required in the first place. It's not fun, but it is part of our job to consider and evaluate this possibility.

Having confirmed the need for a given project, getting on course and staying on course for the duration of the project is key to success. A project is a journey, and as I'm sure you have heard before – one degree off course at the beginning results in many miles off course by the end of the journey. In project terms this means schedule and cost over-runs and possibly outright failure. By the same token, a project that delivers the wrong thing on time and within cost is still a failure.

Figure 1: Project Journey

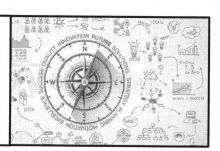

A project is a journey, and one degree off-course at the beginning will mean many miles off-course by the end of that journey. Getting on course and staying on course is crucial to project success.

There are three main elements involved in getting on the proper course:

1. Delivery Strategy

A plain, non-technical statement describing the intended method of delivery for the project in question.

2. Project Life-Cycle

I will not bore our readers with a definition of a project, but I would like to point out a major difference in project management as opposed to functional management. As defined earlier, projects have very distinct phases that they go through. Functional management continues throughout the organization's business life. Projects, however, have specific goals and continue only as long as they are profitable or of some benefit to the organization. It is possible that some projects may transition to Business As Usual (BAU) where they then become operational, but this is not the normal case.

A more comprehensive project lifecycle is included for your review at the end of this book. Various industries and organizations may have slightly different terms or stages, but I think you will find these representative.

Let's explore this a little: I have worked on some very technical projects such as the Magellan Mission to Venus, The Korean High-Speed Rail project, and various upgrades to military aircraft. These are heavily requirements driven projects, and as such, requirements would heavily influence the content of each of the agreed phases. (See the project phase chart in the Appendix.)

For a business transformation program, the technical life cycle is just part of the overall delivery. The important thing about the project life-cycle, is that it must incorporate processes and deliverables that ensure that we build the right things, and that we build the things right.

3. Delivery Execution Model

Projects are essentially temporary organizations set-up to efficiently deliver predefined outcomes and deliverables. Every successful organization has at its heart an optimized operating model designed to suit the industry and marketplace in question.

We call the operating model designed to help ensure the success of a project a Delivery Execution Model (DeMo). The DeMo model is designed to support the agreed Delivery Strategy and Project Life-cycle. The exercise of defining and understanding the DeMo will drive many of the activities in the mobilization plan for your project i.e. everything that needs to be in place to enable your project to operate effectively. (See the Mini Case Study below which illustrates the importance of being clear about the Delivery Strategy, Project Life-cycle, and Delivery Execution Mode.)

Projects are essentially temporary organizations set-up to deliver predefined outcomes and deliverables. Every successful organization has at its heart an optimized operating model designed to suit the industry and marketplace in question. We call the operating model designed to help ensure the success of a project a Delivery Execution Model (DeMo). The DeMo is designed to support the agreed Delivery Strategy and Project Life-cycle. The exercise of defining and understanding the DeMo will drive many of the activities in the mobilization plan for your project i.e. everything that needs to be in place to enable your project to operate effectively. (See the Mini Case Study on the following page which illustrates the importance of being clear about the Delivery Strategy, Project Life-cycle, and Delivery Execution Mode.)

Mini Case Study

Mark was once hired to manage an agile development program. To avoid confusion, in this book at least, we take the industry standard view of a program being a collection of projects.

The price and the duration of each project had been agreed during commercial negotiations against very high-level requirements. He was subsequently briefed that he had 24 months to deliver the entire program.

To make a long story short, the client had never done the relatively new process called "agile software development" prior to this contract. That meant that an agile software development approach suitable for the entire program needed to be documented, supporting tools purchased, and staff trained. The approach adopted needed to be flexible and adapted from pure agile models as the teams were not co-located.

Having hired the team and reached an agreement regarding the development approach, which had to be reviewed with many stakeholders, training for the team was begun, and the first 3 months of a 24-month timeframe was lost in the process. Before work could begin, the team required time to become familiar with the approach and the tools. Only after that could a work rate be established. (Agile refers to this as Calibration). The team was a little slow initially, adding an additional delay of 1 month, leaving 20 months to delivery.

While agreeing to the development approach, it was discovered that the software would be required 5 months prior to the go-live date. This was for internal testing and acceptance procedures (the system used sensitive data) and for training. Now the 20-month window turned into 15 months. The shortened timeframe meant that the team needed to complete much more of the work in parallel than envisaged during the contract negotiation stage, requiring more development and test environments than anticipated.

Having calibrated the team and developed an understanding of how much time was required for development and testing, we estimated that 15 more environments were required, along with 7 more analysts, 10 more developers, and 5 more testers. These estimates included the delay of acquiring and training these resources and procuring and setting up the technical environments, all of which reduced the time for delivery to 14 months. The situation was exacerbated by having to locate the development and test teams in different buildings, as we exceeded the permitted headcount for assigned space. While we did all that we could to minimize the impact, productivity did suffer.

Even though the 24 month program actually had to be done in 14 months, our client delivered 7 of the 9 projects on-time, with the remaining two being postponed indefinitely by their customer. While our client did ultimately produce excellent quality software, because of poor up-front planning, they did not make the desired margin on the contract, having incurred significant extra costs during the project.

Mark Hunt: 2018

Your Team: They Determine *Your* Success or Failure

"None of us is as smart as all of us."
Ken Blanchard

"None of us is as dumb as all of us."
Douglas Fain

Notice that the title says *your* success or failure. That was purposely italicized to make a point. Certainly the team determines the success or failure of the project, but they also determine the success of the project manager as well. It gets very personal, really. If I had a dollar for every time some colleague, client, or student *whined* (yes, I chose that word specifically) that they really had no choice in the team they were assigned, then I would be writing this chapter from a beautiful beach somewhere in Maui. I would be typing with one hand and holding a Mai Tai in the other. And since this chapter is somewhat coherent, you know I'm not in Hawaii and do not have that drink available. The point is, selecting the right team is perhaps one of the most important things you can do to ensure the success of your project (and also success for your own career.) I once knew two very accomplished engineers as they started their careers in a fine aerospace company. Let's call them Bill and Jim. Both were nice men; both were very competent, but they had one striking difference. When it was time to allocate personnel to projects, Jim became a ferocious lion. He would demand certain people, refuse less capable engineers and send them back to their home shop and then call the manager of that organization and scream obscenities until he got the person he wanted. He would pound on the table, call senior management and complain, etc. You get the idea. In time he became known for his insistence on specific people for his teams. Naturally, he didn't always get all of the first-string players he wanted, but he got most of the best the company had to offer. Bill, on the other hand, would accept whoever was assigned and explain that he would do the best he could with the resources he had. How nice. Fast forward about fifteen years. Guess which one had the best record of successes on his projects and became the president of the company while the "nice guy" was back on the drawing boards. I always tell young project managers that they can do more in this area than they think. It may take having lunch with the HR manager now and then, or banging on his door in anger now and then. You simply have to know the people involved and work diligently to get the best team you can accumulate. Most corporations do a miserable job of dealing with poorly performing employees. Someone is always looking for a place to dump the fourth string players. Be aware of the qualifications of everyone assigned to your project and don't accept poor performers. Just send them back to the home shop and ask for a replacement. Once you get a reputation like Jim's, the folks doing the assignments will most likely give you better alternatives just to avoid the hassle you will present. As one colleague once asked, "Would you rather be known as a failed manager or as a person who is difficult to deal with regarding personnel assignments?" I recently read the New York Times bestseller, *Grow a Pair,* written by Larry Winget. I highly recommend it; Winget points to a reality that is often missing in corporate America today. Most great project managers I have known are neither timid nor shy. They also understand the old expression of the chain being no stronger than the weakest link. Take the time to know who your weakest link might be. Should that person receive more training, more oversight, or perhaps even replacement.

After World War II Theory X was the predominant management style in America. That quickly became a concern, and the tough guys were moved to secluded jobs where they couldn't terrorize the neighborhood. Then we moved toward theory Y very quickly. We may have gone too far. I often encounter PMs who are so concerned about being popular with their teams that they sometimes forget they have a project to complete. Establishing the right balance is critical. You need to be fair and thoughtful regarding your team. You also have a job to do. Today all universities seem to be using the "team" approach (sometimes called a *group grope*). Each class is divided into teams for things like reports and presentations. Inevitably some students realize they can get by with little effort since the rest of the team want good grades. (We also have that same situation in our society in general it seems, but that is another story—in one of my novels.) When I got tired of the complaining from the diligent students, I announced that the teams would operate just like businesses (after all, it was a business class)—they could simply fire the person who did not do his/her fair share of the work. I also told them if they didn't have the courage or will to do that they probably should drop out of an MBA program anyway. So the grand experiment began. Over the years I've had five students "fired" by their teams. And then an interesting thing happened. I called each individual who had been discharged by their compatriots and advised them that they were now a team of one. When faced with the situation, not one of them dropped the class. Every one of them got to work and earned an A on their own. Once they realized it was all up to them, they performed well. Perhaps there is a message there that can be used in other areas as well.

We have talked about the quality of the team members that you select. Two other aspects are quantity and technical skills. Do you have enough people to do the work you need to accomplish? Also, do the team members have the appropriate skills to do the work required? I recall years ago when RF engineers were in short supply it was one of the key areas of concern for most project managers managing large telecom projects. Getting the right number of that resource was a very vexing problem for several years. Some of those engineers made salaries equivalent to their division vice presidents. (Thank you Adam Smith—Supply and Demand is still alive and well in the world of business.) But, as with all pendulums, they tend to swing back eventually. The RF engineer shortage was solved relatively quickly as both the demand and supply curves shifted to meet the new environment.

Let me add one more variable that is often missed. Teams are made up of individuals, and individuals have personalities that affect everything they do. So, in addition to numbers of team members and specific skill areas, let's add the human aspect of managing people. Let me give you an example. I have a friend who consults in the field of education. He once relayed a story to me about a company that had a major project they needed to complete successfully and quickly. They determined every skill needed for the project and selected the very best person in their company with each of those skills. Surprisingly, it did not go well. Everyone was a stellar employee, a motivated self-starter, and everyone on the team wanted to be the boss and give directions. As the old saying goes, they were all chiefs with no Indians. I once worked on another project where the company was developing a new product. It also did not go well. It seems the team was made up of all engineers with a particular personality type, but there were no *innovators* in the group. This topic area is a rather difficult one and will be covered in another book to be finished later. (*The Human Side of Project Management*) Knowing how to deal with many different personalities on a project is a skill that many technical managers lack; however, it is a very important area and one that deserves much more attention. As my friend Don Gier says, "Soft skills are the hard part of project management."

In addition to managing one's team, the PM also has to manage his/her customer. I find varying degrees of this skill among most PMs. Some years ago when we were asked to assess a major telecom company's project managers, our team found that they were deficient in two areas. One was the *business* side of the project, and the second was that of managing their customers. This is a key issue if a project is to succeed. I recall once talking to a young PM who told me he had failed on his project. I asked if he had been late or over budget since I knew the project had worked well technically. He explained they had been under budget and ahead of schedule. I was confused. Why did he feel he had failed? He commented that the customer said he would never do business with the PM's company again. He was right; he had failed. I did some research and discovered the reason for the customer's anger. The customer had once been called by his boss's boss to attend a meeting and explain a problem on the project. The customer called the contractor's PM for an update on the project and could not reach him. It seems the PM had a record of not returning calls. The customer was embarrassed in the meeting when he could not answer his senior management's questions and blamed the PM. I later took that young PM with me to meet with the customer (whom I knew), and the three of us had a long talk with many apologies and assurances that the lesson had been learned well. Thankfully, the customer agreed to give the young man another chance. I also talked to another PM on a project that was over a year late and had significantly exceeded its cost target. The customer loved the PM's work and how he explained every delay and said that contractor would get all future contracts. That PM succeeded. There are some major issues here to consider. How often should the PM meet with the customer? What level of status does the customer want? (Some want the 50,000-foot version; others want to get down in the details—customers are different. You need to discuss this with your customer and agree on such things.) Also, be aware, as best you can, of your customer's reporting structure and how she communicates status to her upper management. Ideally, you and she should present the same reports to your respective seniors.

One of our professionals at CEBG, Inc. is an authority on dealing with various personality types. I continue to marvel at her understanding of people and how effective that is in managing relationships. Many times I have considered just how important that skill would be for anyone starting their career. What a powerful tool to be able to understand the differences among people and deal with each in a positive and constructive manner.

Let me take a moment and make a recommendation to all new PMs—especially if you are an engineer: take some time early in your career and learn a few things that might initially be a weakness for you. Take a few courses in finance, contract law, and an excellent personality profile course. Many fine technical engineers fail as managers due to weaknesses in these areas. Also, don't forget the "business" of your project is every bit as important as the technical areas you enjoy.

Managing the *Business* of the Project

"A bad system will beat a good person every time."

W. Edwards Deming

We've shown the importance of developing a great schedule and monitoring performance against it. Another measure that accompanies time is, of course, money. There are several key errors we've seen where money issues have caused major failures on projects. Some of these will be out of the PM's control, but they should not be out of his/her field of view. The first error is starting a project with inadequate funding. Naturally, customers want the work to be accomplished for the smallest price possible. Senior management wants a bid that is competitive and stands a good chance of winning. The PM, on the other hand, wants enough money to do the work and ensure a successful project. I have discussed this issue earlier. I have seen many projects fail due to the lack of attention to the business aspects of the project. Most of the project managers I have dealt with were technical people. Technical experts offer many benefits for the operation of the project. However, the PM must also be aware that there is a totally different set of very complex problems other than technical issues that he/she must manage. A number of clients have used our course in "Project Business Management" to help alleviate this problem.

Let me give one example. Many times engineers and technical people only think of risks in terms of technical issues. In many cases the technical issues are minor compared to business risks. One project on which I consulted had a major risk that could have bankrupted my client. At the final stages of contract negotiations liquidated damages were added to the contract. We had all seen these before, but this one had a risk that most missed. It simply stated that if the project did not complete on a certain date the contractor would start paying liquidated damages to the customer. The problem was that the contractor did not have complete control over the completion date. The project was in California and included the construction of many telecom sites around Los Angeles. Luckily I had worked in California earlier and recognized the problem with building permits. On an earlier project in that state I once asked an engineer how long it normally took to get a permit to construct a tower in California. I recall he laughed and said "somewhere between six weeks and six years." If my friend had signed that contract as written, the risk would have been huge. If the building permits were delayed, the impact to the project could cost the contractor literally millions of dollars. We negotiated a different wording to say if the contract were not completed within three months after the final building permit was issued then the liquidated damages would apply. That was a risk we felt acceptable. This one small point might well have saved the contractor from bankruptcy.

It behooves any PM to carefully study and understand the business side of his/her project. Things like payment terms in the contract are extremely important. If your payment comes six or seven months late, that is a major issue in the financial management of a company, especially a small one. (I once had a contract with one of the largest computer companies in the US where we were paid 7 months after our invoice was submitted. That is a significant problem for a smaller company that has payroll and expenses to meet each month. Unfortunately that happens far more often than most would expect.) It is also wise to review the terms of payment. What, exactly, is required for the invoice to be processed? Is the paperwork and billing procedure clearly specified and understood? And what about subcontractors? How are they selected and managed?

(Subcontractors will be covered in more detail in a later section of this book.)

Risks: They Can Destroy Your Project,
But Opportunities Can Enhance Your Project.

*"The only dumb risk you ever take is the one you don't
know you are taking."*

Unknown

A few years ago I flew to the west coast to sit in a contract negotiation and assist a client I had known for years. I had little time to prepare for the meeting and rushed in as it was starting. After coffee was served we got down to business. My client's customer looked at both of us and said that the $531 Million bid was fine; they would accept our number. I was shocked and asked for a quick caucus. I told my friend that he had obviously missed something. I had never seen a project of that size without days spent negotiating every trivial aspect of the contract. I recall commenting that the customer didn't even want to argue about the pay scales of the engineers. My friend smiled and told me that both he and the customer knew that the risk level in the project was on the order of 40% of the total price. While a percent or two gained in negotiations on a $531 Million contract is a lot of money, the real issue was who better understood the risks. That side would win the negotiation. We then went back, reviewed the project, and began the process of defining and negotiating more risks than I could imagine.

When risks are identified on a project, the PM simply has to make a judgment of its severity and then make a decision of what should be done. There are three basic choices that can be selected depending on the type of risk and the anticipated impact on the project should it occur. They are visualized in Figure 5 on the next page.

Figure 5: Risk Choices

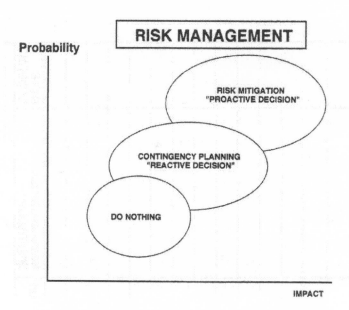

The three alternatives are listed below:

1. Be proactive and mitigate the risk (spend money and resources and reduce the impact or the probability of the risk.)
2. Initiate contingency planning (what to do after the risk occurs)
3. Do nothing! (Sometimes that is the appropriate decision if the risk probability is small or the impact minor.)

In the past we had something called *contingency funds* included in our estimates for new projects. Typically all or part of those funds were deleted as the management endeavored to achieve a more competitive price in the bidding wars that would ensue. Senior management wants to win the contract, and many times that means cutting the estimates considerably. The PM, on the other hand, realizes he/she must have sufficient budget to do the work and ensure a successful project. Let me give a simplified example. Suppose you have the following presented at a Bid Scrub meeting. (This is the meeting where management reviews and approves the bid/proposal that is ready to be submitted to a customer.)

Cost...$10.0 M

- Labor
- Materials
- Travel
- Etc.

Risks...$4.0 M

-Risks (1-n)

Margin.......................................$4.0 M

Total Price..................................$18.0 M

As soon as the bid scrub commences, a marketing expert or a senior level executive will stand and declare that if a bid is submitted for one dollar over $14 M, you lose the bid. At that point, one of the decision makers will automatically place a large X through the $18.0 M and replace it with $14.0 M. Now the fun starts. Contingency funds are the obvious target for removal in the effort to become more competitive. After all, these are funds allocated to illusory problems that cannot be defined and might not happen at all. Later when they were changed to *risk funds* it became a bit more difficult to just delete them in a review. Now the PM had something he/she could defend. (Note the R 1-n. That represents a number of risks that are specified and documented with cost impacts to the project.) While it was difficult to defend *contingency* funds, *risk* funds for specific items could be explained in detail and defended more easily. It didn't take long for the project teams, and the project managers

69

in particular, to realize that contingency funds didn't work well. They would generally be cut in the bid scrub, and there was never enough money to cover the inevitable risks that would arise. This led to a concerted effort to replace contingency funds with risk funds. I can defend the fact that a certain electronic part has never been flown in space before and therefore there is some risk that outgassing or extreme temperatures might impact its performance. I cannot defend a general concept that is simply a title for a bucket of money that has no specific purposes defined except contingencies that *might* arise. So, what is the answer to the simplified example above? Senior management needs to understand how much money is really needed to successfully complete the project. Then, based on that they have a decision to make—how much profit is necessary to incentivize them to submit a bid. In the case above, the profit would most likely be zero. If it is not a strategic project, then perhaps a no-bid is appropriate. (By the way, there are instances where a "no-bid" is appropriate for a number of reasons. Profit is certainly one reason, but sending a message to a difficult customer is another. It is my personal opinion that this no-bid "tool" is not used as often as it should be.)

I always remind PMs that risks (in a business sense) are simply costs with probabilities in front of them. As we have shown, if they happen, you will need money to correct them. So how does one ensure there are sufficient funds to cover the risks that occur. This is where *expected values* come in. Any experienced PM knows you simply take the probability of the risk and multiply it by the financial impact of the risk to arrive at the expected value of that event.

Probability x Financial Impact = Expected Value

Now, that works well—as long as there are sufficient numbers of risks involved to make it statistically viable. Taking this example to the extreme, suppose there is only one risk.

Further, suppose it has a 50% probability of occurrence with a $100 impact. That gives an Expected Value of $50. Should that risk happen, there will not be enough money available to accommodate it. As stated above, there needs to be a risk sample size large enough to make the math work.

Another issue is that of abnormal risk values. If there are 20 risks in the $50,000 range on your project and one at $2 Million, you will have deal with the larger one separately. It simply overwhelms the others in a numerical analysis.

Finally, there is one other key aspect of using expected values for risks in the bidding process that is seldom discussed but should be considered. Some of those probabilities and financial impacts are no more than guesses. Others are good to the third decimal point. Yet we combine them all together—very accurate estimates and those I call guess squared (guess of the probability x guess of the impact = guess squared). There is no scientific way to handle this other than sound, educated considerations and experience. The main thing is to remember what you are dealing with. You may well have a number of your expected values that are little more than guesses, and they are being evaluated with others that are quite accurate; just be aware of that fact.

As a consultant I am frequently asked what a PM should do regarding risks that are not identified before the price is set in stone. That is a very practical question. As I often say, the only dumb risk you ever take is the one you don't know you're taking. The first thing I recommend is that the team do its best job to identify all of the risks. Call in outside help, experts, etc. and pursue the risk identification task with all the talent you can get. The second thing I recommend is that the PM determine that he/she will do everything possible to ensure that the risk funds are not cut in the Bid Scrub. I recall a Bid Scrub early in my career where there was a move to cut the risk funds. I made the statement that cutting the *price* would have absolutely no impact

71

on the *cost* whatsoever. I commented that the costs and the risks were real and most likely they were too small. There were certainly unknown risks we had yet to discover. So, if management needed to reduce the price, they would necessarily have to reduce the margin (profit). This, of course, is not what management wants to hear. But if you can defend each of the risks individually and show that the number in your risk bid comes from a reasonable analysis of the risk table, you at least have a chance of winning.

Now, back to something I said earlier, there are risks we do not know until the project is underway. That is certainly true, and any experienced PM will know what I am talking about. That leads to a statement I make frequently with clients. "Your risk numbers in your bid are too low!" Why? There are risks out there waiting for us that we have not yet identified, and there is no funding for their resolution. There is a famous statement by former Secretary of Defense Donald Rumsfeld that covers this very well.

> "Reports that say that something hasn't happened are always interesting to me, because as we know, there are known knowns; there are things we know we know. We also know there are known unknowns; that is to say we know there are some things we do not know. But there are also unknown unknowns – the ones we don't know we don't know. And if one looks throughout the history of our country and other free countries, it is the latter category that tend to be the difficult ones."
>
> Cited from https://en.wikipedia.org/wiki/There_are_known_knowns#cite_note-defense.gov-transcript-1

I always recommend that PMs be truthful with their management and their customers. However, if you are ever tempted to "pad" the numbers, your risk estimates are the place to start. Defend those numbers in the bid scrub; try to avoid any reduction in them, and increase them if you can. I cannot remember a project that had ample risk funds. There is one other way to increase these funds, but it is not easy. You can make risks a part of your change program and add funds into that area as changes are processed.

I have attended many risk meetings in my life. Generally the team is told to come to the meeting and to bring a list of five or more risks to add to the brainstorming session. In the meeting various team members share their lists, and the items are added to flip charts or whiteboards around the room. Each is then analyzed for probability and impact with a score of *high*, *medium*, or *low*. The key items are discussed, and mitigation assignments are made if needed. I have to admit that in most of those meetings we were sifting through stacks of hay. However, every now and then a diamond is found. I recall a risk meeting on the Magellan Spacecraft project where a young engineer mentioned that he had been reading a scientific report that predicted there would be more solar flares while our spacecraft was in flight than at any known time in history. Wow, we all sat up and took notice. We knew that meant protons flying through space, but no one was certain what that would do to our spacecraft. Several engineers were asked to do some research and then advise the team three days later. As it turns out, the risk was to the computers. Other than those little 1s and 0s, there was no concern. But since the computers were the brains of the craft, we had a problem. We immediately devised a plan to shield the computers, and the mission was a huge success. So all of the boring meetings with little impact were worth the effort to find that one major item that everyone had missed up to that point. We all know the ramifications of bad decisions regarding risks. The Challenger flight comes immediately to mind.

One final thing regarding risks. Do you consider the opposite effect—opportunities. Opportunities are just like risks, except the sign is different; it is a plus instead of a negative. Like risks, opportunities have probabilities and impacts, but if an opportunity occurs, it will have a positive effect on the project, not a negative one. I recall a project meeting for a large software project where a young engineer suggested that if the company were willing to spend another $8,000 in the development of a certain module, there was a 75% probability that the new software package could be used on three new projects in the next year, thus saving about $300,000. This is a good example of an opportunity. (The plan was approved, and it did save the company a large amount of money—I recommended to my client that the young man be given a substantial bonus for his suggestion. I never knew if that happened or not. If it did, I suspect they got even more good ideas from their staff. That was an excellent opportunity to send an important message to employees—we reward good work.)

Opportunities are your chance to improve your project and a thorough development of this process is well worth the time. I see risk assessments on most every project I visit as a consultant, yet I seldom see opportunities discussed or pursued.

There is one special opportunity that is generally missed by most projects. I call it trading. I once worked on a project where the customer badly wanted a change to the requirements. The problem was he had inadequate funds to finance the change at that time. A very sharp project manager recognized the opportunity and negotiated a win-win change order. The contractor agreed to do the new change for free in return for a small change in requirements for a major subsystem on the project. Analysis by the customer's engineers found it to be acceptable, so it was agreed. Completing the customer's change cost the contractor about $150,000. The change in the subsystem requirement, however, allowed the contractor to purchase a pre-existing subsystem (COTS—Commercial-Off-The-Shelf) without the normal development process for a completely new design. It saved the contractor about $2 million and perhaps more importantly, it saved about five months' schedule time. A little creative thinking on the part of the project manager proved highly successful for both contractor and customer in this case. (I recommended that PM for a bonus as well, but his boss said he was simply doing his job. After some thought I recognized his view was actually right. However, I still like bonuses for good employees. That kind of bonus generally brings additional benefits in the long run.)

When risks are identified, it is a good idea to try to eliminate them if possible. The best way to do this is simply not to contract for that risk. In essence, you give it back to the customer. Earlier I mentioned the difficulty in getting building permits in California. Perhaps you could convince your customer to take care of that task since they would have more contacts in that state. Another important risk for many projects today that would be good to transfer to the customer is the Environmental Impact Analysis and Statement. These can take months, and in some cases decades, (think Keystone pipeline) and cost millions! If you cannot eliminate the risks, an option is to mitigate them. Mitigation is spending money to insure the risk does not happen. You may be able to reduce the impact of the risk or the probability that it happens. An example I have seen is adding cable supports for telecom towers (guy wires) to prevent damage from high winds. You should also make every attempt possible to place the risk where it can best be handled. That may be in a sub-contractor's business, or perhaps you might buy an insurance policy or a performance bond. Be innovative. Look carefully to see if you can reduce the probability or the impact, or perhaps even both. I have also seen risks changed to more acceptable forms: schedule, cost, or technical. Capping the liability in the contract is another way to limit the cost of some risks.

One other thought. I once had a client who spent $250,000 to mitigate a risk that would have only cost $150,000 had it occurred. As you might imagine, that was a very interesting meeting when management became aware of those numbers.

There are occasions when someone discovers a major risk that could seriously damage a project. Some define these as things that can injure people or cause a complete shutdown of the project. Needless-to-say, we are talking about serious risks. These are called "Jeopardy Items." There are rules regarding these when they are discovered or identified.

- Report any Jeopardy Item to senior management *Immediately*! (I once recall the president of a major aerospace company telling his engineers that he could bring to bear the entire assets of that company to solve a serious issue—but only if he was made aware of it.)
- Do not delay in the hope that you can get more information and perhaps solve it later. Report all Jeopardy items immediately.

You will find a checklist for risks in the Templates section of this book. I hope you find it useful.

While the topic of another time and book, I feel I should briefly mention complexity theory as it might apply to project failures and especially to the identification and management of risks and opportunities. The following is a good description from a colleague of how that applies.

"Complexity Theory proposes that highly complex systems do not behave in a finite manner but rather their outcomes (behaviors) range across a probabilistic set of possible outcomes. This is fine and can be managed to a certain extent, except as the system approaches its boundaries. Then, the outcomes become erratic and the predictions become extremely difficult. This ties into risk management on very large projects, especially those pushing the edge of technology or operational performance. A much overlooked mantra for managing complexity is: "beware of unintended consequences." In other words, when preparing risk mitigation plans, don't just focus on resolving the particular risk; be sure to examine possible impacts in adjacent areas. You may find that your solution upsets more than it fixes!"

L. Hawkins

Just-in-Time Scheduling

"It is better to do the right thing slowly than the wrong thing quickly."

Peter Turla

I recently sat with a friend from a major automotive company and discussed their recent closing of several plants due to a fire at one of their subcontractors. I found it interesting that the company did not have a secondary supply source or perhaps even a sizable supply of the parts on hand since they were not particularly expensive. I was assured that the auto manufacturer was using Just-in-Time (JIT) practices. My comment was: "How's that working for you?" It reminded me of a consulting assignment I once had where a midsized manufacturing company had been shut down as a result of a certain part that was unavailable due to a problem at their subcontractor's plant. I recall the vice president of manufacturing explaining the situation to his boss during a major staff meeting to discuss the problem. Work had stopped on the assembly line and there were approximately 240 employees sitting on the floor in the manufacturing area—waiting for parts. The company was losing a lot of money as the problem continued. I happen to be there for another reason but had been invited to attend the meeting. Eventually the president of the company looked over at me and asked my opinion as a consultant. I recall asking three standard questions whenever JIT is concerned.

    (1) How much does the part cost?
    (2) Where is the supplier located?
    (3) How much of the supplier's business
         does your company represent?

The cost of each part was 87 cents; the supplier was located in France; and the company represented less than 2% of that supplier's business.

I had noted a large warehouse sitting empty outside the manufacturing area and inquired why there were no spare parts there? Again, I was informed that they were using Just-in-Time (JIT) procedures at the plant. I explained that in Japan, where JIT originated and was practiced so successfully, the situation was much different than in our country. In Japan, the suppliers are almost always within a few miles of their primary customers. In the case of Japanese auto makers, for example, the suppliers are generally nearby and over 90% of their business is with the auto manufacturer they support. If a large percentage of your business is with a particular company, they can be assured that you will resolve their problem expeditiously. The situation that the company executives were discussing in the meeting was considerably different. The supplier in question was located in France, and the percentage of their business that was associated with the company in America was quite small. That is a considerably different situation of how JIT is practiced in Japan. A rather small investment in parts could have averted the disaster they faced. When the finance representative noted the large sums of money being lost, I added that the financial losses were the second most embarrassing issue at hand. The VP of manufacturing asked what I considered to be worse than the financial losses. Before I could answer, the president offered that it was probably the fact that 240 workers sitting on the manufacturing floor were most likely laughing at the "suits" in our meeting. I'm afraid he was right. A rather small investment in spare parts could have easily averted the situation they were facing. There are times when one must analyze standard operating procedures carefully to insure they are appropriate for each company's particular needs. This is an example of a business process failure. The implementation of JIT at this, and many other companies, starts initially as a business process

79

implementation; it is generally planned and executed as a project, tested in a controlled (plant) environment, and then implemented via process change and training throughout the corporation. The failure, in this case, was not in the implementation. That appears to have been successful. The failure was much earlier, in the business requirements analysis phase of the originating project. Had the company analysts thoroughly thought through the consequences of supplier interruptions they most probably would have established a JIT risk/value floor. That is, the most comfortable level of supplier risk versus part value whereby JIT may be implemented. An 87 cent part from a 2% supplier would not have made the cut!

Subcontracting/Managing in a Global Economy

In our careers, Mark and I have been fortunate to have been able to work in over 40 different countries. That has been exciting; it has also created challenges that we have had to learn to manage effectively. This kind of experience is invaluable for professional consultants in today's business environment. As noted earlier, sharing the work is key to today's global economy. It is a good way to reduce risks, save money and/or time, gain access to new technology, and in some cases it might even be required in your contract. Work sharing can be handled on three successive levels, each with progressively higher involvement and responsibility:

1) Outsourcing – buying common parts and/or labor from known suppliers rather than building/performing the work in-house.

2) Subcontracting - assigning (contracting for) a specific portion of the overall effort with another company.

3) Partnering – sharing delivery responsibility with another company. But remember at all three levels, you are the prime contractor, and you own the responsibility. So, know your subcontractors' management skills and integrity as well as their technical capabilities. Reputation is very important—theirs affects yours.

In today's global economy understanding and carefully specifying/communicating requirements are fundamental to the way business is done. Any PM who does not understand that operates at his/her own peril. We have already discussed the importance of clear and well managed requirements on projects. The same is true for the requirements that will be issued to your subcontractor. Vague requirements are a major danger for a contractor; they are equally dangerous for the subs who will act as suppliers for that project. The RFP that is sent to any contractor or subcontractor needs to be carefully constructed. It needs to be clear and comprehensive. Evaluation criteria specifying how the proposals will be scored should also be included in the bid process. Likewise, contracts should be concise and should reference the Statement of Work (SOW) and/or the Service Level Agreement (SLA). Scheduled progress checkpoints and appropriate approvals should be required for progress payments per the contract. A change management process must be established, understood, and included in the contract. Late deliverables and sub-standard deliverables must be addressed in the contract as well. These are some of the issues that must be considered as part of a formal contractor selection process. I once reviewed such a procedure in a client's office. It even included a red-flag warning related to issues that arise due to differences in company sizes, industries, corporate cultures, etc. Upon reflection, I realized just how important these issues could become.

In the past corporations worked diligently to concentrate work in their own company (vertical integration). Today, many companies strive to outsource much of their work and function as an integrator (horizontal integration). Automobile manufacturing is a very good example. It is often the case that the chassis, the motor, and the transmission are fabricated in different countries and then integrated in some plant in Alabama. This allows the principle of specialization to add value to the process, but it also adds numerous potential problem areas if not managed well.

In the past decade a new job function has arisen that is growing in numbers and also importance. That is the position of Subcontract Manager. I once worked on a project that had work being done in every state in the US and seven other nations as well. It was a huge project ($4.5 Billion) and the scope of the work was staggering. Our Subcontract Manager was responsible for more budget than most corporate CEOs in the country at that time. His responsibilities were enormous. He was responsible for subcontract requirements, contracts, deliveries, testing, reporting, scheduling, etc. etc. His responsibilities were second only to those of the overall project manager.

The performance of the subcontracting effort on any project is often key to that project's success. How well it is managed will determine to a very large degree the overall success of the project. Selecting a strong individual to lead that effort is extremely important and should be done early in the life of the project. Long lead procurement and the volume of work that is generally needed makes this essential. As subcontracting continues to grow in the current business environment there are numerous new issues that will arise. Communications, configuration control, international laws and regulations all enter into the normal mix of management challenges. Sometimes the issues are totally unexpected. An example occurred several years ago when a major spacecraft failed in space. It was later discovered that the engineering included both metric and English measurements; they were not consistent. When I heard of the error, I did not believe it. Since I had spent almost twenty years in that industry, I called some friends to confirm the reports. Their answer I received was that a lot of red-faced engineers were still trying to determine how that mistake had been made. It was all part of the international nature of the project. Various parts had been made in different locations around the world and the measurements simply didn't match. It is hard to imagine how that error occurred; it is even more amazing that it was not caught in the exhaustive testing program.

As explained, subcontract outsourcing is an area that needs professional management in order for the project to be successful. You may want to refer to our Consultant Checklist for the template regarding managing outsourcing successfully.

I recently taught a graduate level course in procurement at the University of Denver and am convinced that this area is one of the greatest challenges facing new managers today. Numerous texts have been written regarding the role of procurement on large projects; the ones I've read were excellent. I highly recommend that new project managers become very familiar with this increasingly important area of our business.

Project Control: Ensure Things Happen Per Plan

Once the project has been initiated and the work is underway, the key issue then becomes one of completing the project per the schedule and the budget. (It is also nice if it does what it was intended to do technically as well!) As a consultant I have reviewed many projects where failure came as a complete surprise late in the process. How does that happen? How does failure sneak up on a project team? (I could include the customer in this as well. I would expect the customer to be somewhat involved in the project as it develops, especially in the case of cost-plus contracts. After all, it is the customer's money that is being spent or wasted.) I have already addressed the subject of project planning (and how poorly most projects are planned). But there is a second phase of planning that is often overlooked—project control. This is what I call the second half of planning—ensuring that the things that were planned happen as planned and things that were not part of the plan do not happen. First you build a good plan, then you manage that plan to ensure the work is progressing as you anticipated.

I have seen numerous techniques for maintaining control of projects. The technical changes are typically managed through a Change Control Board. The budget and schedule are either managed individually or in combination via some type of Earned Value system. There will be some who argue that there is only one Earned Value system, but as a consultant, I have seen several adaptations, and on one occasion I helped develop a system we dubbed "Earned Value Light." The customer wanted an EV system but could not afford the complete version. (When I was on the Magellan Mission to Venus project we also had some budget issues that required us to pare down the total EV system my company typically used. The new one we developed was cheaper, and it worked.) What was needed was some way to ensure that budget and schedule goals were established and being met in a realistic, measurable fashion. I cannot count the number of times I have heard "We are on schedule and on budget!" when everyone knew it was doubtful that was true. If your schedule is three months old with no changes or updates, you can be sure the schedule status is at best a guess. Yet, I have seen such schedule reports drive other groups to work overtime in order to maintain a schedule date that was most likely unrealistic. An example? How did the recent federal healthcare website get to the launch phase with no one knowing it had problems and would fail? Surprise! Who chose that contractor?

A few quick comments about Earned Value. Typically, this is new to most commercial companies. Aerospace companies, on the other hand, have used this for many years and are quite adept at its implementation. For those new to the joys of implementing a full-up Earned Value system, let me offer a few words of advice.

1. Earned Value is not easy and it is not cheap. It will require that you train the entire team in your EV system. (And that really means everybody—you can't do it with just a few people.) This training will require professionals who know the system well. They will train the team, but you will necessarily be the one who convinces the team that this is essential and important to the project's success. (I recommend a vice-president or a high-level director of the organization be the one to make that speech to the team.) Engineers are not typically fond of things like Earned Value, so some salesmanship will be necessary.

2. Setting up the computer systems to link schedules and budgets in the EV system is not a job for a beginner. You will need professional support. I like to call them *cultists*. These are consultants who have earned a very good living helping companies set up EV systems, and

they are a bargain if you are about to embark on this journey. Trust me, you will eventually need them, so start smart and bring them on-board immediately. There are pros out there who do this well. Hire one.

3. Don't underestimate the cost of your Earned Value system. If you are bidding a project with EV as a requirement, you will need to do some serious thinking about the budget required for that effort. (good time to call the pros)

4. Earned Value cannot work well without a good schedule. You may recall my earlier comment that few projects have good schedules. Enough said.

5. You need to know why you are moving toward an EV system. Is it because the customer requires it on your project, or is it something your company wants to try. If your situation is the latter, you are now going to have to sell your customer on this idea as well as your team. (Remember, this system is not cheap. It is very expensive.)

6. Some people argue that EV looks backward. In other words, it measures progress that was accomplished a month or more in the past in some cases. One way to solve this criticism is to do the EV measurements every two weeks rather than the typical monthly update. That would help the backward view issue, but it would also increase the costs of keeping the system running. Remember, EV requires all of your team's participation. You don't want to violate Fain's third law of management: "If you spend more time reporting what you are doing rather than doing what you are reporting, you are doing something wrong." You want your engineers doing engineering work, not processing paperwork, and extensive record processing is required of all team members using an EV system.

Regardless of the control system you choose, there are several key items you must keep in mind. One of the first is deciding what you need to measure. On the Magellan spacecraft, one of the key items we measured repeatedly was *weight*. The weight of the spacecraft was, perhaps, one of the biggest concerns on the project. If that value were not correct, we would not be able to get to Venus or get into the correct orbit around the planet. So, ask yourself what things need meticulous care and measurement in order for your project to succeed. Certainly schedule and budget are important as are the technical requirements on the project, but are there other things like, perhaps, weight, or CPU usage or memory usage in large scale software projects, that are also key to your success. How will you manage and control them? How frequently will measurements need to be made? What are acceptable values? How will you handle values out of tolerance? What kind of status meetings will be held to report status on those items?

Every project is different, but I would recommend at least a weekly status meeting where project performance is measured and discussed. Build a Responsibility and Accountability Matrix (RAM) where tasks are assigned to the responsible personnel. Agree on schedule dates and then hold regular status meetings to ensure things are progressing as planned. This is also a good time to hold the project Action Item meeting. The program planner typically runs this meeting with the PM in attendance. Important actions are noted and tracked to ensure that things are being done per agreement and schedule requirement. There are numerous forms that can be used to track action items, but I would suggest that you ensure the form allows tracking of all "promise" dates for actions that are not completed as agreed. One other suggestion. The dates on the schedule and the action item list are dates negotiated and agreed to by the person who will actually do the work. If the PM simply assigns all the work and the dates for accomplishment of the various tasks, there will be little "ownership" by the team members. I would also suggest that the action item meeting and any status meetings be held in a Management Information Center (MIC), a room where the project schedule is available on the wall. Typically the schedule is used to a large degree during these meetings. The MIC is also a good place to post important artifacts that assist in managing the project. (project action items, equipment lists, key milestone dates, RAM, etc.) Take down your pictures of sailboats and beaches and put things on the wall that will help manage your project. In today's world of global contracting and performance, a virtual MIC can (must) be set up that can be securely accessed from remote locations. Also, it is a good idea to be aware of time zone differences when setting status meetings. My good friend, Len Hawkins, as an additional duty to being Group Vice President of Engineering for a major international aerospace company, chaired the corporate Engineering Process Council. As such, he hosted, at his headquarters, quarterly process standardization and improvement working sessions. To keep costs down and boost attendance by representatives from the world-wide business units, Len initiated a virtual meeting environment, whereby people could participate in a visual and web-based conference. The challenge became: Its 8:00 AM in Washington DC, but its 5:00 AM in Los Angeles, 5:00 PM in Abu Dhabi, 1:00 PM in London and 11:00 PM in Brisbane! Some folks had to adjust their work schedules but is was still better and cheaper than attending in person.

Communication

"Listen with curiosity. Speak with honesty. Act with integrity."

Roy T. Bennett

No discourse on failed projects would be complete without a section on communication. This is an area that has plagued mankind for centuries. Likewise, it has been the downfall of many projects as well. One could go into a very lengthy discussion of this topic; it could well be a volume of its own. I will instead cover the specific project related communications that cause difficulties for those trying to complete a specific job with a myriad of constraints along the way.

The first area of project communications that must be addressed is that of dealing with one's customers. We have spent time already covering this from the aspect of determining the objectives and the requirements of the project. Let me repeat a few important items regarding requirements. When you are working with your customer to establish requirements for a project, this is some of the most important work that will be done to achieve a successful completion of the job. These requirements must be documented and their configuration managed carefully. I have found that people tend to forget some of the agreements they make. This could be intentional or unintentional, but it happens.

Since we are discussing customers, let me address this topic a bit further. There are some individuals who feel they, as customers, have little to do with the actual work of a project. (This is definitely not the case on large government cost-plus contracts. Unlike fixed price contracts, the government customer with a cost-plus contract has a very well-defined role, and also they know that it is their budget that is being spent. On a fixed price contract, the costs are established and well defined; on a cost-plus contract expenditures are initially indeterminate, so it behooves the customer to participate in the management of the work.)

On many projects, and especially in-house projects, the individual customer may fail to realize that he/she has a very important role to play in setting the requirements of the project. These requirements will determine the cost and the schedule of the project and also the technical performance. A customer once gave his contractor the specs for a trailer he wanted built. The contractor built the trailer as specified, but it became evident that it was not big enough to carry the product the customer wanted to transport - obviously a mistake by the customer. As a colleague stated, if this had been a government project, the customer would have been promoted; the contractor would have been blamed but would have gotten a bonus; and the taxpayers would have effectively paid for two new trailers.

Most everyone involved in project work understands the three key issues on any project: (1) Technical Requirements, (2) Budget, and (3) Schedule (I always like to add customer satisfaction as well). On most projects one of these will be the project "driver." This is the key issue that drives the project for the customer. It is essential that the project team understand this in order to first win the business and then to satisfy the customer. I will discuss this later, but it is key on every project that the project team understand this clearly. If the schedule is the issue for the customer, a low bid will most likely not win the contract. I once sat in on a bid review and a young contractor stood before my client and explained that his bid would be the highest price the customer would see that day. The reason was that he had added extra equipment and personnel to ensure that the schedule would be met as planned. He had numerous great ideas to accommodate any risk that might arise to threaten the schedule. It was expensive, but it was assurance that the schedule would be met. The other bidders came to the meeting and emphasized their low bids. They lost. The schedule was the driver for that particular project. On another occasion I received a call in the middle of the night from the VP of a major telecom company. She needed me in Tampa the next day to help resolve an issue with their software. It seems it was not collecting the data needed to charge their customers for long distance calls. (Remember "long distance" calls?) She never asked my consulting rate; she just told me to be on the next plane. Once again, it was a schedule driven project. When you are losing millions in revenue each day due to a software glitch, the issue is to fix that as soon as possible. Three days later they were back on-line. The money paid to the team members was insignificant compared to the revenues that had been lost.

Another element of requirements and customers involves a job some project managers do quite well and others do not—carefully managing customer expectations and perceptions. As mentioned earlier, one of our clients had us study their project managers and measure their proficiency in a number of areas. One of the items we discovered was that their PMs were not as skilled as they should have been on the "business" side of the project. They were great in the technical arena, but they were quite weak dealing with business issues. They also had another weakness that we discovered and spent some time correcting. The project managers in that company were almost entirely technical people who were not nearly as skillful as one would hope in dealing with customers, in setting and managing expectations and perceptions.

I know there are those who would dispute the following

argument, but I have seen enough examples of successes to refute the excuses I continue to hear. (The first big excuse in project management is "I have no control over the resources assigned to my project." The second is "I have no control over my customer.") The project manager can, and should, influence the perceptions and the expectations of his/her customer. Again, I know this to be true because I have seen some excellent project managers who do this very well. One of the areas where this skill is particularly important is in the development of project requirements. Dealing with unreal requirements or vague requirements can be an important part of any PM's job. Helping the customer understand and appreciate the importance of real, detailed requirements is one area where the PM can practice that skill with great results. We actually developed two courses for project managers needing more training. The first was "How to manage your customer in a project environment." The second was "Project Business Management." Several organizations have used those courses to improve their customer relationships and also to improve business performance on their projects.

Let me address one other important issue regarding managing customer expectations. Expectations tend to drift as the project progresses. There are many reasons for this, but the key is to understand that this is "normal," and you can therefore plan for it and minimize the damage this could cause. Consider the following. As a project begins we can assume there is basic agreement about the work and how it would proceed when the contract is signed. All of the differences from the negotiation process have been resolved and there is general agreement on the work to be done. The following chart illustrates this situation. Initially all are happy with the contract as it proceeds.

Figure 6: Expectations Model

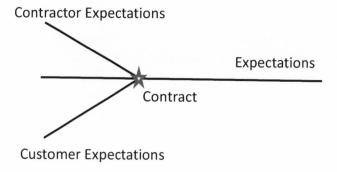

But over time, expectations begin to drift—for both the customer and the contractor. I typically hear things like: "The customer doesn't have a clue what we are trying to do. All they do is get in the way." Then I hear customers say things like: "All the contractor does is nickel and dime us to death. They really don't care about anything but the money." So expectations begin to diverge as illustrated on the following chart.

Figure 7: Diverging Expectations Model

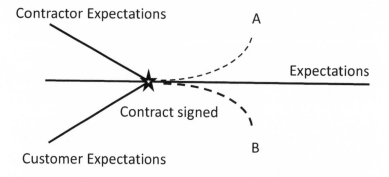

If we know this is a natural tendency and will most likely happen, it behooves us to avoid the problem by taking steps to bring the parties back together to ensure they remain in agreement regarding the goals of the project and how we intend to achieve them. One of the best ways to do that is to have regularly scheduled meetings to review all of the major aspects of the project together. These might be in the form of a Design Review, a TIM (Technical Interchange Meeting) or a PMR (Project Management Review). When these are held, it facilitates returning everyone's focus back to the objectives of the project. It is an immediate opportunity to improve communications and trust as well. Expectations drift is real and a common issue that all project managers need to be aware of. Understanding and anticipating this phenomenon is the first step in preventing the damage it can cause to your project and to your customer relationships.

Figure 8: Corrected Diverging Expectations Model

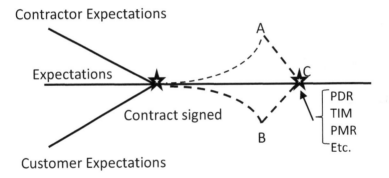

Be aware, however, as soon as that meeting is held, expectations will start to drift again. As stated, this is normal. Both sides will most likely experience this same phenomenon. Don't become angry with your customer/contractor; instead, meet on a regular basis and avoid this situation. Most large contractors have recognized this over the years and have regularly scheduled events with their customers. It is a good practice to follow.

I have also found it useful on some projects to keep detailed records of all communications with customers. On one project early in my career, the project had special forms on pink paper that were to be used for phone conversations with certain customers. We actually took notes while we talked. Those were promptly sent to the PM who reviewed each and then filed them for future reference if needed. (Most projects won't need this, but if your relationship with your customer necessitates this, it is a handy tool to verify status items, agreements, disagreements, etc.)

The suggestion for managing customer and management communications with regularly scheduled meetings can be facilitated with various project reviews. These begin with the Project Initiation Review with your own management personnel at the beginning of the project, a Kickoff meeting with your team, and a Contract Initiation Review with your customer. After the project is in operation, PMRs (Project Management Reviews), Technical Interchange Meetings (TIMs), status reviews, etc. should be held regularly with your customer and your management. These typically have established formats that do not change. Topics typically include things like (1) Major project issues, (2) Schedule status, (3) Budget status, (4) Technical status, (5) Significant Action Items. Keep the format consistent so the participants can easily track changes. These meetings take time, but they afford an opportunity to communicate with both your customer and your management and keep them apprised about the status of the project. (Note: I once used this on a project that was "in-house." I added one very important slide to the presentation. It was titled: "What I need from you." My boss smiled; he had been a project manager as well and understood the reason for that information. This leads to one of Fain's laws about project management: You can delegate upward as long as you meet certain rules:

(1) It has to be an action that you cannot do alone—it is above your grade level.

(2) It must be a task that your boss is capable of doing —i.e., he/she has a high enough position in the company to make such a decision.

(3) Without this action/decision, the project will fail.

Use this sparingly, but when you need it, it works with most bosses. If it doesn't work with your own boss, start working on your resume. You need another boss.

Most project managers work diligently to communicate with their customers. Unfortunately, some fail to remember that their senior management are also customers. Many companies have their own format for meetings and reports regarding project status. Use those well; take the time to ensure they are accurate and prepared professionally. If your organization doesn't have such communication channels, sit with your boss and establish one for your project. It is good for the project; it is good for your own career as well.

One other caution regarding communication with your customer and your company upper management, be sure that your message is clearly communicated, as necessary, up both management chains. On one very large government project, which was a partnership between two major aerospace companies, this communication failed spectacularly and with job consequences for both partner project managers. The project involved the software system for a combination hardware, software, and infrastructure initiative. It turns out that the government agency heads for each of the elements of the program were bragging to one another about how their element was

97

succeeding. When the hardware and infrastructure elements ran into trouble, the executive in charge of the software element started crowing about how his element was "on-time" and "within budget." Unfortunately, that wasn't entirely true! The project managers for both companies had been reporting to the on-site customer and their respective company upper management for two months that the budget was being underrun and the schedule was in jeopardy and might experience a six-month slip due to test failures. That information failed to make it up to the agency head until the quarterly combined Executive Review. When the situation was briefed to the combined element executives it came as a tragic surprise to them all, and was a major embarrassment to the software agency head! The result was that both company project managers were removed, and the agency head lost significant credibility.

We've discussed various ways to communicate with meetings and reports. I would suggest that for the project kickoff meeting you prepare and distribute a form that lists all of the recurring meetings and reports on the project. List the name of the meeting/report, what will generally be covered, who attends the meetings or receives the reports, who will prepare the report, and when meetings will be held, or reports distributed. If inputs are due from members of the team, list that as well and when they are due. You may be surprised at the amount of confusion this will eliminate on your project. One other suggestion regarding reports, if a form is required, distribute both hard and soft copies (put it on your project server). I tend to add an example of the report as well. That way when you say you need schedule status from each area, they will know if you mean milestones, a schedule, or a written report explaining how things are going. On many occasions these reports will be aggregated for a report to senior management. Make it easy for the person doing that work. If he/she receives consistent formatting, it is much easier to compile the project's status.

Great project managers learn very quickly that you cannot effectively manage a large project from your desk. If the PM is spending more than a couple of hours each day on his/her computer, there is a problem. I like the term "management by walking around." You need to be where the work is. That gives you an excellent opportunity to talk to the team members and understand their problems. They see the project from an entirely different perspective from the management staff. Chatting with team members is a great chance to see that other perspective. It also is an opportunity to motivate and reward your team. Everyone, everyone, likes to be told they are doing a good job. (P.S., Beer and pizza or coffee and donuts are cheap.) Fain's first law of business is: "If you can make those working for you successful, they will make you successful as well." Actively search for ways to encourage and reward your team members, but be sure your rewards and recognition are genuine for actual performance that is exemplary.

I would recommend any new project manager take a good course in communications. Most big companies have those available. I have also found that understanding non-verbal communications is a great tool as well. Any tool that assists us in this huge arena of communications is useful. One last comment for new PMs. If you do not write well, hire someone on your team who does. It is essential that all written communications with customers and senior management be professional. This is important for the project; it is especially important for your career. I have seen a number of cases of great technical managers who were passed over for promotions simply because of perceptions that grew out of poorly written reports. Don't let this happen in your career. (I would like to see more courses in written communications and interpersonal relations added to more college engineering core curriculum. Many would find it helpful in their careers.)

Contracts

"What does the contract really say?"

Sign over the door—Charlie Brown's office (not from the comic strip. Charlie was my boss for several years, a senior manager at Martin Marietta Aerospace.)

There is yet another area that occasionally causes difficulties on projects. This one falls squarely into the realm of the business development folks. It involves contracts and the legal side of any business. Contracts are the foundation upon which business is done in many countries, certainly it is true in the United States. (But be aware, contracts are not held in the same esteem in all societies.) Understanding your contract is essential for any successful business. (That is why we have so many lawyers driving BMWs and Jaguars.)

I'd like to focus on three distinct issues for contracts:

(1) Choosing the right contract type for a project is important.
(2) Managing the special problems of international shipments requires special attention.
(3) Dealing with the different international views of contracts and what they represent, interesting international negotiating techniques, and how contracts are implemented in various cultures are important topics for all managers.

There are many types of contracts available. The most common are depicted in the following table:

Table 1: Types of Contracts

Contract Type/risk	How it is used
Cost only **Client risk**	These types of contracts are generally used by organizations like universities. The organization completes specified work and receives reimbursement for all costs.
Cost Sharing **Risk shared between client and supplier**	This type of contract is used when participating organizations receive benefit from the work and agree to share the costs. It is used frequently for things like research and development work.
Cost-Plus a Fee **Client risk**	There are various ways to determine the fee involved in this type of contract, depending on how the contract is written. This type of contract is generally used for development work that is new and difficult to estimate. The contractor doing the work is reimbursed for all costs and a fee system is devised to determine the profit that will be made. Note: the fee system can vary considerably among contracts and even within a contract.
Fixed Price **Supplier risk**	Fixed Price contracts are generally used for low risk bids where the work is generally well understood. When the work is completed satisfactorily, the contractor receives an established price.

All of these are viable types of contracts and meet specific needs. It is when the purpose of these types of contracts are misunderstood that projects can get into trouble. Each of these have specific strengths; they each have weaknesses as well. The PM who does not appreciate both can be in for a major surprise. It is a lesson that can become a very expensive education. The biggest area of concern on most projects I've reviewed is choosing between a Cost-Plus and a Fixed Price contract. Strangely, there are many misconceptions about these two contract types. Cost-Plus contracts generally have a bad reputation in the general public. Uneducated people will accuse companies of using these contracts to "fleece" the government. The truth is that Cost-Plus contracts were developed by the government, not contractors. Any good business person knows you can make a lot more profit on a Fixed Price contract if you know what you are doing. I spent almost 20 years working for a major aerospace company as a young engineer. I recall most of our profit levels were in the 5-6% range (many were actually bid at 0% profit)—certainly not enough to entice a commercial company to bid on that kind of work. But why, you might ask, would the government develop a Cost-Plus contract? Actually it was done to protect government agencies financially. Cost-Plus contracts were designed for projects that cannot be estimated accurately. Let's say the government asked your company to bid on developing a space suit for an astronaut to wear on the moon. Since you had not done that before, your estimates might range from something like $1 Million per suit to $10 Million per suit. Until you got into the process, you would not be able to ascertain the actual cost. What would you bid? Certainly not at the lower end of that scale. Most companies would probably bid above the top number—after all, every company has to make a profit in order to stay in business. So, to preclude the contractor from bidding at the top of that estimate scale, the government agrees to pay for all costs of developing and building the suits, plus some fair profit for the contractor. Since there is little risk in such a contract, the word "fair" generally means a very low percentage of profit. Now, let me dispel a modern misconception of these contracts. Most uninformed people assume that the contractor has a great deal and cannot lose money on the

102

contract—not so! I once saw a "fee arrangement" like the one indicated on the following chart.

Figure 9: Fee Arrangement Figure

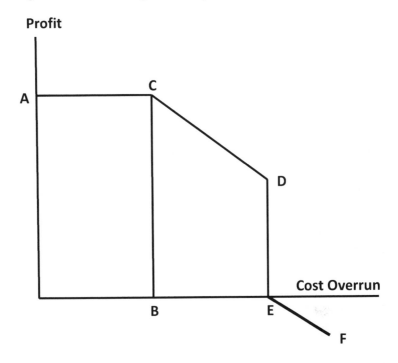

As you can see from the chart above, the contractor will earn a profit of A as long as the "cost overrun" (this is the amount the project actually costs over what was originally bid) is less than B. As the cost overrun exceeds B the profit slides down the line C—D (this is typically called the "slippery slope.") Note that when the cost overrun exceeds E, the profit is actually in the negative zone, and the contractor is essentially paying the government for the privilege of doing the work. (Note that this is also a career limiting event for the contractor's PM team.) It is best to avoid these situations if one has aspirations of advancing within the contractor corporation. As this indicates, it is possible that a contractor can, indeed, lose money on a Cost-Plus contract, depending on how the contract is structured.

There is one other concern that must be addressed in determining the appropriate type of contract to be used. If the Cost-Plus type is chosen, it has very distinct requirements for the customer that are sometimes misunderstood. For example. If a company signs a Fixed Price contract to build a widget and deliver it on a specific date for $100,000, the customer can sign the contract and go on vacation. (The customer's concerns are somewhat limited to two things: (1) Can the contractor build the product to specs, and (2) can the contractor deliver on schedule. The financial risk is essentially gone.) What about a Cost-Plus contract for the same product? Now the contractor is spending money from the customer's bank account, and there is little to limit what is spent. In the case of a Cost-Plus contract, the customer becomes a very active team member on the project. He/she will need to monitor the work on a daily basis to ensure that his/her money is being spent wisely. I recall the representative for the government on the Magellan Mission to Venus had an office near mine and sat in every significant meeting we held. He was involved in every major decision. It worked well, but it required his attention and participation. Customers who don't recognize that fact take unnecessary financial risks and may well end up with a very negative view of their contractor's activities. This is not only a risk to the project but also to future relationships with that customer. The PM will do well to insist that the customer become and stay involved in major decisions on a Cost-Plus project. He/she will protect the company's reputation and future business by insisting on customer involvement, and a wise customer will want that level of participation.

There is another obligation that falls upon the customer in all contracts but can have especially serious consequences in the case of cost-plus contracts. The customer's contracts manager/administrator must carefully control her technical representatives' tendencies to make ad hoc changes during development. Most large government development contracts have customer engineers on-site, generally to monitor and advise but sometimes to participate in the development. These folks are generally dedicated, knowledgeable professionals, who want the best product (system) they can get. This is understandable, but if left unmanaged, this can also lead to out-of-control changes that will drive the cost sky high and may even crash the requirements.

As explained earlier, in the last few decades the world has seen an explosion of international trade. A significant amount of that flow of products and services is used to support major projects in all countries. This brings up another area of significance for any PM involved in a project that has international shipments. The paperwork involved in transferring products across borders is far more complex than one might imagine. I recall a client with a shipment of electronics that were being shipped to a plant the client owned in Mexico. These parts were being expedited to the plant as quickly as possible to protect a shipment of integrated parts to another plant somewhere in Asia. When the trucks reached the Mexican border, they were promptly impounded. As it turned out, the paperwork stated the electronics were made in America—a part of the NAFTA treaty. On the shipping boxes, however, it clearly stated that the parts were made in Thailand. Oops! It was a costly delay.

As I have stated earlier, most Project Managers are from the technical arena. They may understand the technical requirements for the project in great detail, but few have an understanding of the requirements for international rules and paperwork regarding international shipments. Companies that do this regularly usually have a Contracts Administrator who handles all of these details. Successful projects have such support. Those that do not may well end up with significant delays and inflated costs as a result. Another reason a contract administrator is so valuable on international projects is to understand and manage the legalese within these international contracts. As stated earlier, we do business by contractual agreements in America and most of Europe. That is not the case in some other regions of the world. If your customer doesn't give the same value to contractual agreements as you do, it is wise to know that and have a plan to manage any risks that might cause.

One last contractual issue for PMs, and it is an important one, involves a request from the customer for a "minor change" to the T's and C's (terms and conditions) on a contract. NEVER change the T's & C's. We are technical or business people, not lawyers. It is very difficult for us to understand all of the legal implications of those legal notes. The standard answer for such a request from the customer is that as a PM you do not have the authority to make that legal decision. It will have to be analyzed by your company's legal department.

See the Project Contracts checklist in the Appendix for more information.

Leadership

"Management is doing things right; leadership is doing the right things."

Peter Drucker

When I taught the Advanced Project Management course for Stevens Institute of Technology, I always looked forward to the module on leadership. Along with a number of colleagues, I helped develop that course, so I know it well. I always refer to leadership as the glue that holds the team and the project together. As a consultant I have witnessed many projects fail and an equal number succeed simply because of leadership. I once consulted on a project that had a poorly developed plan. (I keep repeating that fact—most projects are poorly planned—sorry, that is just a fact.) That project, however, succeeded simply because the team was determined that they would not let it fail, and they would not be late. It involved many late hours and considerable overtime (unpaid on that project) just to ensure success. If I had been the boss of that section, I would have given all of them a good bonus and then hired several good project planners. Similarly, I once witnessed what I considered to be one of the finest plans I had ever seen on a major airline. I recall thinking I was standing in the presence of genius as a director explained his new plan for airport operations. Unfortunately, it failed. The reason? He was not able to explain the complex plan to the union shop steward who kept saying "I'm not sure this will work." (What he really meant was, "I don't understand this.") After the shop steward protested several times, the director became irritated that the union official could not recognize the genius on the sheet before him. That finally led to angry exchanges, and then the shop steward stated flatly, "I'm sure this won't work!" And it did not.

Had the director spent more time understanding where the shop steward was coming from, it might have gone much differently. Sheer technical genius failed before the alter of human ignorance. There was a good lesson to be learned from that experience. Technical genius is wonderful, but understanding people is key to achieving success in most human endeavors. Another condition that thwarts good leadership is ego. Good leaders know they may not be the smartest person on the project, but they know how to get the best performance from their people. They recognize who has the knowledge and understanding of a particular situation and how to clear the way for that person (or team) to get the work done. Note: This is not "leading from behind," this is pushing ahead, out front, clearing away obstacles, roadblocks and potholes to enable the team to be successful!

When I begin to analyze a project's situation, especially those that have failed, I like to ask myself some basic leadership questions:

1. Is there a charismatic, inspiring leader on the project who will lead from the front and by example, one who lives and breathes the *raison d'etra* of the project.

2. Does the leader live and die by his/her decisions and is he/she willing to bet his/her career on what he/she says and does and delivers every day?

3. Does the leader paint the big picture and show everyone where they fit in and how to relate their daily tasks to each of the deliverables of the project? (Knowing why you are doing what you are doing is a great and comforting motivator.) Breaking down the big picture into recognizable pieces with well understood components and content is part of creating a visualization of the project, its deliverables, and the end game.

4. Do the team members feel a personal ownership for the project's success or failure?

5. How mature is project management in the organization? How does the project manager deal with that answer?

   a. Is there a project life cycle developed that integrates with the current organization and its processes that explains the business interfaces at both ends of the cycle—how you get into the life cycle, what you do within the life cycle, what the deliverables are, and how do you get out of each phase of the life cycle.

   b. Has the organization approved and instituted an approach, common ways of working, and the tools and processes necessary to manage a project even when multiple organizations are involved.

   c. Is there a Project Management Office established within the organization? What do they offer the project teams? What do they expect from those teams?

6. How well does senior management understand project management in general, and how well do they understand each particular project and its peculiarities? Perhaps more importantly, how well does senior management support projects and PMs? Are upper level managers also leaders?

One of the finest project managers I ever worked with eventually became a corporate CEO. His skill at project management was balanced by a keen understanding of people and how they work and think and interact. I am always a bit dismayed at the number of project managers who tend to be so skilled at the technical aspects of the business but so woefully inept at dealing with members of his/her team and especially his/her customers. While there are certainly many wonderful examples of engineers who are skilled at handling people, dealing with other humans is normally not a talent that tends to gravitate to the technical elite. In today's environment, engineers who are inspirational leaders are in great demand.

I was recently asked about the characteristics of a great leader. As I pondered that question I recalled a certain combat mission that would require flying at a relatively low airspeed and a very low altitude up a very steep canyon. The enemy gunners would actually shoot down at us as we flew by. All smart pilots dreaded that particular valley, dubbed *Rat Fink Valley* by the pilots. On one particular morning as we briefed, our flight lead, an older and very experienced Lieutenant Colonel looked over to see that we had a new lieutenant flying with us on one of his first combat missions. He was as green as the proverbial gourd. The colonel thought a moment and then stated that when we entered the valley, the lieutenant would take the lead and fly up the valley as number 1. The colonel would follow at the rear as number 4. Most of us in the room knew why. By far, the preponderance of the anti-aircraft fire would be focused on the third and fourth aircraft. Number 1 and number 2 would wake up the gunners as they passed, who would then be ready for the last two aircraft. I'm fairly certain that lieutenant did not understand the change in the flight order until later that day. But I'm sure he never forgot the lesson of true leadership from a man he could trust and look up to for the rest of his career. (Colonel Bennett, I salute you, Sir!) I never had the opportunity to fly with Robin Olds, another legendary fighter pilot, but the respect he earned from his men has been seldom matched in Air Force history. He was a leader of men. (For more on this subject, you might try my award-winning novel, *The Phantom's Song.*)

For many years there has been an ongoing discussion regarding the differences between management and leadership. They are very different and distinct skills. I suspect most all of us have worked for a boss at one time or another who possessed one of these sets of skills but was lacking in the other. Perhaps Peter F. Drucker said it best.

> *"Management is doing things right;*
> *Leadership is doing the right things."*

110

On occasion we are lucky enough to work for a boss who is gifted with both sets of skills. In my own career in the private sector, Frank Borman at Eastern Airlines and Earl Cook at Martin Marietta were men who inspired employees like me to aspire to greater performance and higher goals in our careers. They were exceptional men and outstanding managers and leaders. I was lucky enough to also consider both of them friends.

As mentioned earlier, in my consulting career I have discovered that one of the great weaknesses many have in the technical field is that they are not particularly well trained at dealing with other people, but there are several personality measurement tools like the Enneagram or the Myers Briggs personality profile, etc. that you may find useful. Trust me, we may never become as adept in one of these as we would wish, but they do teach us several good lessons. (1) Not all people are wired the same way, and (2) That is okay. I have worked with individuals who are very skilled in this area and have been amazed at their power of understanding how to deal with others more effectively. Be aware, this is not a tool for manipulative purposes, but rather it is a tool that helps us understand both others and ourselves better. As I have watched people skilled with these tools operate in business I must have said or thought a thousand times that I wished so much that I had known this skill as a young man starting my career. (I will add that it is also a great skill to have when dealing with teenage children, spouses, bosses, etc. as well) I know of two particularly sensitive contracts that my company, CEBG Consulting, won simply due to great advice on how to deal with our customers more effectively. As you can probably tell, I am a firm believer in this aspect of managing our customers and our employees more efficiently. It makes everyone's life easier and more productive.

Failure to Identify a Suitable Delivery Strategy

Deciding how the project can be delivered

Having assured ourselves that the project is valid and has support from the organization's leaders, there are big gains to be made simply by agreeing, in a plain English statement, just how the project can be delivered e.g. for a project designed to improve a company's product to market time the project will:

1. Map the current business processes involved in the new product introduction
2. Identify opportunities for improvement
3. Review these with stakeholders and prioritize
4. Design a new product introduction process
5. Perform an impact analysis against the current operating model
6. Identify the affected processes, systems and organizational changes required to support the new process
7. Produce a next steps plan and seek required approvals

Socializing this with stakeholders will help to uncover any issues with the proposed approach and identify other stakeholders. We must not overlook stakeholders!

Failure to Identify a Delivery Operating Model

Define the operating model required to deliver the project

If considered in terms of what it really is, a project is, in effect, an operating model that will result in the work required to deliver the project being completed.

It is clear that we are going to need time with various subject matter experts from a number, if not all, of the functions within the business. Data personnel, business and systems analysts, and business and systems architects should all assist in designing our proposed solution/s.

We must define the operating model that supports the Delivery Strategy. The team is going to need a common way of working, both in terms of a business and technical project lifecycle supported by the appropriate processes, systems, and training if they are not familiar with these, and they also need time to form, storm, norm and perform. Consideration must be given to the stabilization of the team, the time this will take, and the anticipated work rate that can be achieved.

All of the above will need to be established at an appropriate level to enable the project initiation to begin. "An appropriate level" means scaled according to the stage in which the project is operating.

From the above we can envisage that there is going to be an analysis, design, build, test, and implement type of approach and that there will be a technical lifecycle required within the business lifecycle of the project. There will also be significant change and communications work required to implement the new product introduction process.

Then of course there is the unforeseen. At the start of a project, when we are working out how we may achieve what we are setting out to deliver, we are not aware of all of the complexity that is hidden in the details. It may be necessary to conduct feasibility studies, run complicated procurements, or discover a new set of requirements to inform our decision regarding the most feasible delivery option. Note: While diligence and discipline will be required to analyze and then address the unforeseen, essentially what you will have done is identify the known unknowns. On every project, there are unknown unknowns hidden from view and just waiting to interrupt your plan! Be aware of this and try to build slack in your schedule and contingency in your budget to accommodate these circumstances.

Before any code is developed, any business processes are reviewed, or any real effort is expended, there are many considerations to be analyzed to address each area of the project in question, holistically. These must be thought through, a way forward agreed upon, the steps required to set the project up to succeed identified, and a mobilization plan built.

Ethics

"Ethics is the foundation of your most important professional possession—your reputation."

Douglas Fain

I have taught project management for corporate clients, colleges, and graduate students in fine universities for a long time. One area I always cover is that of ethics. Perhaps the greatest area where this comes into play in project management is in status reporting. There are cases where project managers give bad progress reports due to ignorance (the schedule was not worth the paper it was printed on) or perhaps it was intentional. Either way, if the status given is inaccurate, in time the reputation of the individual, and perhaps even the organization, will be tarnished. Avoid that. One's reputation is the most important asset he/she has in his/her career. The same is true for organizations. Protect it well. I once watched a director of a very large company taken out of the workplace early one morning in handcuffs. (There were many engineers standing at the windows of the engineering building watching in shock.) The individual had been caught intentionally falsifying cost reports for a rather large project. (The government was paying the bills and they were monitoring the money carefully!) Being arrested by the FBI is certainly a career-limiting move. Don't ever do something like that.

I recall another instance of a director in a major aerospace company lying about the status of engineering on a very large project on which he was working. The PM on that particular project was also a corporate level vice president in that company. When the PM realized the director had lied about his organization's performance status, the PM demoted the director to manager and replaced him on the project. It was a lesson no one missed. You don't lie about status on a project. Decisions are being made every day that depend on the accuracy of status reports. If the PM cannot trust the truthfulness of his/her team, it could be very difficult to manage effectively. I have noted in my international travels that there are some countries where truthfulness is not as highly regarded as a virtue as others. In those countries where lying is more acceptable, I have noted that the standard of living is generally lower. Veracity is important in business. It impacts your ability to manage, and it is key to your reputation as a professional.

One way to ensure successful reporting on a project is to establish a strong set of progress metrics. These should cover more than just time and budget. They must address workflow, technical productivity (e.g., lines of code or object definition on software projects), operational modeling, testing, etc. A good set of metrics will keep reporting leads "honest" and show a project manager where to focus his attention.

One of the best pieces of advice regarding ethics comes from a talented professor in a small Jesuit College in Denver— my wife. She once told her students that they should take time in the quiet of their own homes to sit and think carefully where they stood on ethical questions. Where did they draw the line they would not cross? Consider that carefully, she told them. Then file that in their minds forever. She noted that many good and decent people have found themselves caught in a rushed meeting where they were asked to make an instantaneous decision that they had not considered adequately. Sometimes they made the wrong choice because they were surprised in the moment. I think this is excellent advice. Know where you stand. Know what you stand for. Know where your line in the sand really is. Then confirm in your mind that you will not cross that line under any circumstances. As one colleague once said; "Better to lose your job than to lose your integrity."

Project Closeout

"One test is worth a thousand expert opinions."

Werner Von Braun

At the end of most projects everyone is anxious for the work to be finalized. There are new assignments to be initiated and perhaps even a vacation to be taken with the family. Everyone is ready to close the books and move on to the next challenge. (That is true for writers as well I might add—especially if the writer is an engineer!) Yet, I have seen many projects encounter significant problems at this phase of the work.

Let me first address the actual completion of the project. That is generally accomplished with some form of acceptance. This happens when the project team demonstrates that the project will do what it was intended to do in the contract. This may be demonstrated with something called an Acceptance Test (I prefer using the term Acceptance Demonstration—a test implies testing until something fails. That is not the purpose of an acceptance demonstration.) A few thoughts on acceptance:

1. The acceptance criteria must be developed at the outset of the project. Develop these early and have them signed, as part of the contract, by both the contractor and the customer. DO NOT wait until just before the acceptance demonstration to outline the criteria that signifies successful completion. If you do wait until later in the project, I can assure you the acceptance criteria will grow substantially from what it might have been had it been prepared earlier. Customer consultants like to add tons of requirements for the acceptance test at the last minute. These add cost, time, and risk of failure. Decide early with the customer what the acceptance test should be, and make it a contractual document. Any changes after it is established must go through

118

the CCB (Change Control Board). That way any additional testing added at the end of the project will add cost to the customer. This generally tends to reduce the last minute additions.

2. When the acceptance test is complete, your customer may suggest that you get together later to complete the paperwork. (This is especially prevalent when the test ends at 2:00 o'clock in the morning.) Don't agree to that. Have the paperwork completed/ready and ensure someone has documented any issues that may need further work on a punch list. As soon as the test is over, hand the customer the proper paperwork and have them sign it. This is to avoid having additional items added later. Your customer may well have a consultant observe the demonstration. He/she will need to add something to show that his/her fees were worthwhile. You want to complete acceptance as quickly as possible so you can invoice the customer and get paid. (Remember the points about the "business" of your project?) So have the Certificate of Completion (and punch list if necessary) available for signature as soon as the test/demonstration is complete.

3. Be careful that your acceptance test punch list does not include problems that are not actually a part of the acceptance test. I have seen occasions where some customers will try to add warranty items or contract change items to the list. Keep these separate. You may have a punch list of items from your demonstration (test) that needs to be resolved. You may also have other items that are not part of the acceptance demonstration that need to be resolved as well, but keep them separate. It does not look good to have a lengthy failure list from your acceptance test. Sometimes this is simply a place where outstanding items can be documented, but sometimes this might be used to gain freebies at the contractor's expense.

After the project is complete, a Lessons Learned exercise is a great tool to discern what did not go well and what was successful. The key is to avoid making the same mistakes on future projects. I recommend three lessons learned sessions. The first is with your own project team. What went right? What went wrong? What did we learn? What would we do differently next time? Then I suggest holding a session with the customer to review similar things. What could we have done to make the process easier for the customer? What would the customer have liked to see us do differently? Etc. Then, wait several months and revisit the customer with a couple of your key personnel. This lets them know you care about their success. How is the project working for you? Is there something that would make it work better? How can we support you better? You may even want to do a bit of positive marketing while there. Did your cellular system get enough coverage on the north side of town where all the growth is happening? Would it be beneficial to add a few more towers in that area? Etc.

Finally archive all of your records from the project. You never know when a customer will have a question about the project in the future. I once had the government ask about the schedule status on a project I planned seven years earlier. We were able to locate the schedules that showed the status two days before and one week after the date in question. That impressed them and filled their needs.

One last point about closeout. This is the time to ensure your team are reassigned to another good project. It is also a time to reward those who deserve special acknowledgement. I recall once walking into a finance department's employee ranking session. They looked at me and wondered what a technical manager was doing in a finance meeting to assess their personnel. I told them that the finance representative on my last project was particularly efficient and deserved special mention, and I was there to do that. I advised them that I would wait until his name came up for evaluation—then I wanted to speak. They had never seen that happen in the past. An engineer speaking for a finance person? That day my team member moved up significantly in his ranking, and soon everyone knew I was serious about taking care of my people. (That was very beneficial, it turns out, when I next went searching for a team.) They worked hard for me; the least I could do is return the favor for them.

Back to the project's *business*. I once walked into a client's office and inquired how one of their projects that I had worked on had fared. It had been a big technical success they reported. As we were leaving one of the planners noted that the only thing that had not gone well was that they had not yet received the final payment. I stopped the group and asked the size of that missing payment. $23 Million! It had been a little over six months that the payment was delinquent. I was aware that at that time my client was paying about 15% cost-of-capital. So, 15% x 6 months x $23 Million would equal $1,725,000. Everyone in the room was amazed at the size of their loss. I asked why the payment was late, and no one knew. After a day or so researching the payment it was discovered that a spares report was required in the contract and had never been submitted. That was a half hour job, and it had cost the company almost $2 Million. (I rest my case on the importance of our Project *Business* Management course.) A note: At the beginning of any project have the contracts folks prepare a list of all deliverables and post that on the wall in the Management Information Center. Then status it as the project progresses. At the end of the project it should have initials and dates on every delivery. Avoid late payments due to late deliveries. It is an unnecessary and costly mistake.

Part 2
Managing for Success

"Success usually comes to those who are too busy to be looking for it."

Henry David Thoreau.

Projects vary in scope and complexity, but there are some basic functions that all projects share. It is essential that project managers understand these and the basic process of how projects are developed. Hopefully a better understanding of these will enhance the chances of success.

Below, I present a general overview of project management by mapping the tasks to be accomplished to the phases that most commercial projects share. The list I define is not totally comprehensive, but it should give the reader a basic understanding of how projects are developed, executed, and closed. Most portrayals of this process begin with the contract award after some kind of bid process and subsequent award. I shall go back to the initial idea for the project and follow it through to completion. Note that I present a large, complex commercial project for my outline. Smaller, less complex projects can simply delete the items that are not applicable. One additional point needs to be made with respect to government projects. All government entities, be they federal, state, or local have formal acquisition regulations that the acquiring agency is bound by law to follow. This is true in every country. These regulations vary greatly from country to country and entity to entity and can drastically affect the flow and life-cycle of a project. When bidding and performing government projects, the project manager must be aware of, and adapt to, the regulatory environment within which the project will be accomplished.

In my example, I break the phases down into the following:

- **Concept/Product Study Phase** – (Pre-acquisition work)
  - User requirements definition
  - Concept definition
  - System specification
  - Acquisition planning

- **Acquisition/Implementation Phase**
  - Source Selection
  - System Implementation

- **Operations Phase**
  - Deployment
  - Operations / Maintenance

- **Deactivation**
  - Resolve environmental issues / State requirements
  - Dispose of any hazardous materials
  - Update lessons learned reports
  - Complete punch list / warranty items
  - Submit invoice to customer / pay subcontractors
  - Reassignment of team members

Note: for the person who will be managing an assigned project, you may want to go directly to the Operations Phase for items required to manage your project. It will be useful to understand the entire project life-cycle, but for your immediate concern, you might well skip the Concept and the

Acquisition phase as those will be completed when you receive your assignment.

1.0 Concept/Product Study Phase

For many large and complex projects, it is advisable to do preliminary work before the customer sends a RFP to the various contractors who may wish to bid on the work. There are several reasons for this. First, the customer may well realize that they do not have sufficient knowledge to establish a reasonable set of requirements for the contractors to bid on. It may be that the customer has limited knowledge about the details of the technical issues involved. It may also be that the project is something entirely new and therefore no one knows enough to establish reasonable requirements. (The first mission into space might be a good example.) Secondly, there may be alternatives involved in the work that cannot be determined without extensive research. This, then, requires a study phase to establish requirements that optimize the project's chances of success. (We had a similar study phase for the Magellan Mission to Venus, for example.) This phase is commonly identified by a separate contract that may be issued to several of the contractors simultaneously. After the study phase is completed, the customer has the opportunity to establish a much improved set of project requirements.

1.1 User Requirements Definition

1. Prepare a complete list of all stakeholders who will be users of the project's products.
2. Collect user requirements from ALL stakeholders.
3. Prepare preliminary Project Requirements Document (PRD)
4. Validate requirements with all users in a System Requirements Review (SRR).
5. Measure User requirements against the organization's Strategic Plan.
6. Present project to upper management and secure

project champion and commitment for resources (Project Charter).

7. Review organization lessons learned from similar projects and initiate risk and opportunity assessments. Develop initial Risk / Opportunities Log.

8. Prepare initial resource list and submit Resource Request to appropriate organizational unit. (Note: this may be a "home-shop" or even the HR department in the organization.)

9. Develop models for the system environment and operational environment as necessary.

10. Establish Project Change Control Board.

11. Determine user's operational environment.

1.2 Concept Definition

1. Determine candidate concepts and operational scenarios for the environment selected.

2. Review the candidate concepts and assess the technical feasibility of each.

3. Measure concepts' impact to current operations.

4. Select best concept and prepare System Concept Document.

5. Study concept, build preliminary WBS and prepare estimates for the following:
   a. Total project cost (*Should Cost* at this point)
   b. Time phased funding
   c. Schedule requirements
   d. Staffing requirements
   e. Facility needs
   f. Special requirements (security, etc.)

6. Define preliminary System Acceptance Plan and review with stakeholders.

1.3 System Specification

1. Establish design criteria for the system objectives within cost, schedule, and risk constraints.
2. Determine scope and methods for qualification and acceptance verification.
3. Establish external system interfaces and secure signed Memorandum of Agreement from external entities.
4. Prepare System Specifications for the following Design
   a. System functionality
   b. Quality requirements
   c. Performance requirements
   d. Quality
   e. Technical interfaces
5. Review specs with key personnel and baseline.
6. Trace system specifications requirements in Project Requirements Document.

1.4 Acquisition Planning

1. Determine acquisition strategy:
   a. Act as Prime?
   b. Participate as an Associate?
   c. List of subcontractors.
   d. Use of consultants.
   e. If government contract, determine GFE/GFM/Govt. sites/facilities.
   f. Assess appropriate contract type (Fixed cost, Cost-Plus, etc.)
   g. Will an Earned Value system be required?
2. Prepare list of potential bidders and assess capabilities.

3. Confirm funding profile to support project.

2.0 Acquisition/Implementation Phase

During this phase the customer is involved in the process of selecting the contractor who will do the work on the project. There are several types of contractual documents that can be used, depending on the industry and the type of project to be considered. Some companies even use sequential bids in order to reduce total costs. For example, they may use various combinations of the following:

> RFI – Request for Information
> RFQ – Request for Quote (typically used for materials
> or standard rate labor pricing.)
> RFP – Request for Proposal
> BFP – Best and Final Pricing

Often an RFI is issued to secure information from potential bidders and the information gleaned from that effort can be incorporated into the development of a better RFP.

2.1 Source Selection

Selection process:
1. Prepare Preliminary Request for Proposal (RFP) and send to potential bidders for review and comment. Include the following:
    a. Source selection schedule
    b. Bid instructions
    c. Statement of Work (SOW)
    d. Evaluation criteria
    e. Customer requirements (technical and business)
    f. Appropriate contract information
2. Receive bidder inquiries and respond as appropriate.

3. Conduct team review of RFP.
4. Establish Source Selection Board.
5. Establish Proposal Evaluation Team.
6. Determine Sole Source selection items and prepare justification reports for each.
7. Update RFP with bidder comments as necessary.
8. Confirm funding available.
9. Release Final RFP to bidders.
10. Bidders complete and submit proposals.
    a. Assemble proposal team.
    b. Establish proposal venue.
    c. Collect appropriate materials.
    d. Build schedule for completing the proposal.
    e. Meet with key stakeholders and agree proposal strategy/key issue (Cost, Technical, Schedule, other).
    f. Develop Win Theme.
    g. Contact appropriate subcontractors and include in the bid process as applicable.
    h. Prepare project schedule.
    i. Write proposal.
    j. Determine cost/budget numbers.
    k. Team review of total package (This may happen several times during the proposal process—typically called Red Team, Gold Team, etc. reviews.)
    l. Verify responsiveness to RFP.
    m. Ensure preliminary Acceptance Plan is included in proposal.
    n. Present proposal to "Bid Scrub" team
    o. Update and deliver to customer on time.
11. Customer reviews competitive bids and submits questions as needed.
12. Evaluate proposals and announce winner.
13. Notification sent to bidders who lost.
14. Complete evaluation documentation.

15. Contract negotiation
    a. Bidder and customer assemble negotiation teams.
    b. Both teams review competitive history of the other.
    c. Both teams assemble personnel data relative to the other negotiating team.
    d. Both teams develop negotiating strategy, caucus codes, and "walk-away" points.
    e. Hold negotiations and settle.
    f. Document negotiations and agreement .
    g. Both sides sign contract.
    h. Review long-lead procurement and authorize as necessary.

2.2 System Implementation Plan

Update project Implementation Plan
1. Meet with upper management and propose personnel for project team. Insist on great people!
2. Assemble team and review contract and all specified requirements. (copy of contract for everyone)
3. Meet with negotiation team and review "hot items" from negotiation proceedings.
4. Meet with customer and agree on recurring status meetings and reports. Questions/answer session for all.
5. Determine control gates for the project and get concurrence from management and customer.
6. Update project network (schedule) (entire team participates) and get commitment from team (Note: the schedule developed during the proposal process is most likely inadequate after

the negotiation process concludes. It will undoubtedly need updating.)

7. Update/establish all other project plans:
   a. Project Management Plan
   b. Risk Management Plan
   c. Resource Plan
   d. Financial Funding Plan (Funding Profile)
   e. Quality Control Plan
   f. Configuration Control Plan
   g. Change Control Plan (set up Change Control Board CCB)
   h. Project Acceptance Plan
8. Provide copy of all plans to customer and get customer approval and commitment.
9. Meet with upper management and prepare fee/profitability plan (Company confidential).
10. Compare Risk Plan to schedule critical path and take appropriate action as necessary.
11. Initiate subcontract procurement.
    a. Update subcontractor list.
    b. Negotiate final contracts.
    c. Secure detail schedules for subcontract work and incorporate into project plans.
    d. Subcontract manager meets with subcontractors to review technical, schedule, and cost specifics/goals.
12. Select Design Concept and System Architecture.
13. Identify all configuration items.
14. Analyze System Design Risks.
15. Update System Verification Plan.
16. Develop detail HW/SW Architectures.
17. Develop Plans for system/configuration Item "build-to" and "code-to" documents/inspection plans.
18. Verify Design meets system specifications.

19. Prepare verification procedures for system and configuration items.
20. Develop project maintenance procedures for system and configuration items .
21. Build and perform testing for component HW.
22. Develop and test SW code .
23. Assemble configuration items (Components to sub-assemblies to assemblies, to final configuration items, etc.)
24. Finalize Verification procedures and get signature from customer.
25. Prepare maintenance materials and procedures for HW and SW items.
26. Document "As-built" engineering.
27. Configuration items progress through qualification testing.
28. Ensure all changes are being documented in CCB.
29. Assemble System (HW and SW).
30. Conduct system qualification testing.
31. Complete Operational System Verification.
32. Document "As-built" engineering configuration.
33. Prepare for system shipment to customer.
34. Prepare system deployment plan.
35. Review/update operational training plans.
36. Complete Acceptance testing and documentation (If not required to be accomplished on-site).
37. Hold lessons-learned meeting with team/ subcontractors.
38. Hold lessons learned meeting with customer (wait three months and hold another meeting with customer after system has been used to review performance and additional needs that might have arisen.)
39. Submit invoice per contract.
40. Celebrate with team, subcontractors, and customer.

3.0   Operations Phase

During the Operations Phase, the project is deployed, tested, accepted and begins operations. (Note: depending on the contractual agreements, this may be completed by the contractor as part of the project, or it may be completed by the customer separate from the project contract.) All contract deliverables are verified, and the system is put into use. Training is completed, maintenance procedures are in place, and beneficial use is clearly documented. System updates and enhancements are made as planned or requested. Finally, system deactivation is planned and carried out.

3.1 Deployment Phase

1. Perform site survey and prepare plan for receiving the system.
2. Develop plans for system transportation and implementation.
    a. Transport vehicle, route, environment and safety requirements must be specified.
        i.   Will the travel environment meet product specifications? (heat, cold, g-forces, etc.)
        ii. Are all safety requirements met?
        iii. Are there special permits required?
3. System installation
    a. Physical inventory of all parts/ Audit to ensure all contractual deliverables are delivered.
    b. Install equipment available.
    c. Trained installation personnel assigned
    d. Insure quality control personnel involved
    e. Proper installation documentation on hand

4. Acceptance testing (if not performed earlier)
    a. Insure all Acceptance procedures are complete and signed.
    b. Conduct demonstration/test per contract
    c. Secure certificate of completion of "Conditional Acceptance."
    d. Develop signed Punch List and schedule for completion.

5. Training
    a. Insure all training plans are complete.
    b. Implement training program and document.
    c. Secure training certificates as required.

3.2 Operations and Maintenance Phase

1. System Validation
    a. Finalize system validation procedures.
    b. Conduct System Validation (User Acceptance).
2. Operate the system.
3. Perform System Maintenance.
4. Continue training as required.

4.0 Deactivation Phase

1. Insure deactivation plans and procedures are updated.
2. Determine any environmental issues/state requirements.
   a. Dispose of any hazardous materials.
3. Store/sell/dispose of any remaining materials.
4. Update lessons learned.
5. Hold in-house and customer post-project reviews
6. Complete follow-up punch list / warranty issues
7. Invoice the customer
8. Manage reassignment of team members

Project Templates

(The consultant's checklist)

- Requirements
- Project Qualification
- Risk analysis
- Pro-Forma P&L
- Planning
- Control
- Project Greenbook
- Change Control
- Project Reviews
- Outsourcing
- Project Contracts

These are questions we ask ourselves as we begin an analysis of any project.

Requirements Management

1. Are the project objectives clearly understood and were they communicated to all stakeholders for review and agreement?

2. Are the objectives documented and managed under some kind of configuration control system?

3. Were all stakeholders identified, and were they involved in the requirements process?

4. Is the requirements document(s) comprehensive and complete? Does it contain a large number of TBD's or TBR's? Were there "fuzzy" requirements included in the list? Were details missing? Were the requirements measurable?

5. Was a Systems Requirements Review (SRR) held, and did the owners of the requirements present their list? (Never let the Systems Engineer or the Project Manager present a list of requirements prepared by the stakeholders. The stakeholders should present their own set of requirements. I'll discuss this in more detail later)

6. After the SRR, were the project requirements formally baselined in a PRD (Project Requirements Document) and signed by all parties?

7. Is there a formal process for changing requirements throughout the project, a Change Control Board (CCB)?

8. Were the team properly trained to administer the requirements process?

Project Qualification Template

1. What is the business category of this project? Is it strategic?

2. Strategic Projects:
   - Why is this project strategic?
   - What is the future opportunity?
   - How much is the company willing to invest in this project?
   - How does this project integrate with current business?
   - Are teaming agreements required? With whom? What is our history with this "partner"?
   - What are the risks involved?

3. What resources are required for this project?

4. Do we have the capability to handle this project?

5. Is the project fully funded? Can the customer get funding? Financing?

6. Who is the competition for this project?
   - What are their strengths? Weaknesses?

7. Has the business case been prepared? Approved?

8. Has a project manager been assigned?

9. Has a win strategy been established and reviewed by management? What is the win theme from the proposal?

Project Risk Template

1. Has a risk management plan been established and implemented?

2. Has a senior team member been designated as lead for the risk management program?

3. Are risk management meetings scheduled throughout the project to review risk management? Are the appropriate technical and management people consistently attending?

4. Is risk identification a primary emphasis on the project? Is it rewarded?

5. Are risks on the agenda for all PMRs and TIMs?

6. Is risk assessment/impacts assigned to team members and incorporated into project planning?

7. Are risk mitigation activities identified, planned, budgeted, and managed? Are risks retired in a timely fashion, according to project phase?

8. Are subcontractors, associate contractors, functional support areas, and customers included and held accountable in the risk management program?

9. Are opportunities also included in the risk management process?

Project Pro-Forma P&L Template

1. Is the work clearly defined in a SOW?

2. Are all customer requirements identified/ defined?

3. Are all tasks understood, planned, estimated?

4. Have the SOW, WBS, project plan, and task estimates been reviewed by a Red Team (a team of high level managers in the organization who will monitor and finally approve the proposal/bid)?

5. Have all risks (opportunities) been identified for all phases of the project? Have they been prioritized and priced? Are the probabilities and impacts identified? Does the Red Team Agree?

6. Has all subcontract work been clearly defined and reviewed? Has the company Make/Buy procedure been followed?

7. Has the project category been established for the project? Is it defendable?

8. Has a business case been prepared and reviewed? Approved?

9. Has an adequate competitive analysis been performed?

10. Is the profit level appropriate for the project category selected and the competitive environment

Project Planning Template

1. Are the project requirements understood and baselined?

2. Has the customer signed the project requirements document (PRD)?

3. Have the following been completed and baselined?

   - Project Products list/equipment list
   - Statement of Work (SOW)
   - Work Breakdown Structure (WBS)
   - Master Schedule
   - Network Diagram (major projects)
   - Responsibility/Accountability Matrix

4. Have all of the above been signed by the customer and appropriate levels of management?

5. Is the Critical Path clearly defined and understood?

6. Have the resources been loaded into the plan?

7. Has the network been integrated with customer/other contractors/subcontractors/etc.?

8. Has the team's commitment been secured? (Key Item)

9. Have the appropriate detail schedules been prepared? Do they support the network/master schedule?

10. Do all detail schedules integrate among themselves?

11. Has a formal schedule review been held? (Red Team Review)

12. Does a written change control procedure exist for schedules?

13. Is the project schedule a part of the agenda for all Project Management Reviews?

Project Controls Template

1. Has a project plan been developed and baselined?

2. Are the project risks understood? Documented? Is a risk management plan established?

3. Have the key project items necessary for control been identified? (Key measures for success)

4. Are procedures in place that allow visibility of performance of the key measurement items?

5. Are standards/measures of success identified? (Acceptable standards of performance)

6. Are the measurements of performance taken at appropriate time intervals?

7. Are performance variances reported to the appropriate levels of management?

8. Are corrective actions established? Documented as action items? Tracked on a regular basis?

9. Are the project controls/metrics updated at frequent intervals?

10. Is the value of the information you are receiving worth the cost you must pay for it?

Project Greenbook Template
(Project Information Document)

1. Project Calendar – 2 months

2. Project Schedule – 1 page master schedule

3. Top Ten problems – with resolution plans

4. Top Risks and Mitigation plans/status

5. Project Actions Items-with responsible individual and promise completion date

6. Customer Action Items

7. Formal Review action items (System Design review (SRR), PMRs, Design Reviews, etc.)

8. Appendix:
   - Current reference data – for a limited time
   - Important team communications – for a limited time
   - Engineering release matrix – as applicable
   - Site construction/integration/optimization matrix
   - Build/code software schedules – as applicable
   - Test procedures/test status/etc. – as applicable

Project Change Control Template

1. Is a company/project Change Control Procedure established? Communicated?

2. Has the customer agreed to the change control system? Is it a part of the contract?

3. Is a firm contractual relationship established with an approved SOW, WBS, and project network?

4. Are technical, schedule, and budget baselines established? Documented? Placed under official change control?

5. Has the Change Control Board (CCB) been established? Are the appropriate members notified?

6. Are all team functions represented on the CCB?

7. Are all changes logged and tracked?

8. Is the appropriate approval process established? Is it followed?

9. Are all impact studies integrated among the various disciplines?

10. Are appropriate profit levels incorporated into the pricing of changes?

11. Are cumulative changes reviewed as a regular part of management reviews?

12. Are approved changes communicated effectively with the entire team?

13. Are subcontractors involved in the change process? Are changes effectively communicated to them?

14. Has the team commitment been secured? Is management support in place and obvious?

Project Review Template

1. Project Data Sheet
    - Project name/customer
    - $ value/type of contract
    - Schedule parameters
    - Brief description

2. Customer relationships
    - Prior business/business relationships
    - Size of project relative to customer's base
    - Criticality of project to customer
    - Special customer needs/concerns

3. Requirements
    - Requirements identified, documented, approved
    - Baseline established, approved
    - Change control process established
    - All interfaces identified and included in requirements management
    - SRR (System Requirements Review) complete/documented

4. Engineering design status
    - Is the system architecture complete/approved?
    - Has an architecture/requirements traceability analysis been performed?
    - Is the architecture technically and financially feasible?
    - Can this architecture be completed on schedule?

5. Hardware development
   - Design complete
   - Detail schedules complete
   - Make/Buy approved
   - Manufacturing plans complete
   - Procurement plans complete
   - Test verification/validation plans complete
   - Schedule status

6. Software development
   - Software development plan established
   - Software schedules established
   - Software procurement plan established
   - Software test plans complete
   - Schedule status

7. Integration/test
   - Are all subsystems identified for integration?
   - Is the integration plan complete?
   - Is the test plan complete?
   - Are the test facilities/equipment identified and scheduled?

8. Schedule status
   - Is the WBS established? Approved?
   - Is the project network completed? Approved?
   - Is the critical path identified?
   - Are the lower level detail schedules established and statused as necessary?

- Is the schedule integrated with all subcontractors/ customers/etc.?

9. Management status
   - Is the project manager identified/designated by upper management?
   - Is the organization chart approved and published?
   - Are the personnel assignments adequate? Is additional training necessary?
   - Has a management reserve plan been established for the budget?
   - Is there a plan for communicating on the project?
   - Is there a regular action item meeting scheduled?
   - Are the proper management reviews planned?
   - Is there a management succession list?

10. Risk/Opportunity status
    - Has a risk management plan been established?
    - Are all risks identified?
    - Are opportunities identified?
    - Are risk mitigation plans established?
    - Are contingency plans established?
    - Do the subcontractors and the customer have risk plans?

11. Cost and schedule status
    - Is a cost/schedule status plan established?
    - BCWS/BCWP/ACWP developed for Earned Value tracking?
    - Is tracking and statusing frequency adequate?
    - Is the current EAC established?
    - Is the schedule communicated throughout the project?

12. Contractual status
    - Are terms and conditions approved?

- Is change control operational and documenting contract changes?
- Are all subcontracts completed and approved?

13. Top Ten Project Concerns
- Are the major project problems identified along with resolution plans?

14. Review of assistance needed from upper management
- Is management aware of specifics of needed assistance?
- Has commitment been given?
- Is performance to commitments being monitored and reported?

15. New business opportunities
- New or revised requirements/new technology/enhanced performance/ increased capability.

Project Outsourcing Template

1. Does the company have outsourcing guidelines? Have they been followed?

2. Has a project "Make/Buy" analysis been performed/approved?

3. Has "Sole-Source/Competitive" selection been approved?

4. For sole-source contracts, is justification adequate? (schedule/cost/technical expertise?)

5. For competitive bids, have the proper subcontractors been notified?

6. Were the requirements in the Request for Proposal (RFP) submitted to the subcontractors correct and complete? How often were they changed or updated?

7. Is the procurement cycle compatible with project needs?

8. Does the subcontractor have the technical expertise to manage the subcontract? Do we feel confident that the sub can handle the technical work to our specifications? (This can be a problem on a spacecraft with 1/10,000 inch tolerances.)

9. Has a "should-cost" analysis been

performed? Did the subcontractor estimates agree with our should-cost values? If not, why not?

10. What is the driving factor in this subcontract? (Schedule, Cost, Technical)?

11. Have we done business with this subcontractor before? What was the performance last time? (If it was not good then, why do we expect it to be different this time?) What is the subcontractor's reputation in the industry?

12. Does the subcontractor have the resources to handle a job this size? Are they comfortable with our schedule requirements?

13. Are subcontractors involved in the change process? Are changes effectively communicated to them?

14. What risks are associated with this work? Is the subcontractor aware of the risks? Does the subcontractor have a plan for risk management?

15. Will the subcontractor team with us on items like R&D requirements?

16. Are our engineers and manufacturing people in contact with those of the subcontractor? Are our folks comfortable with this company?

17. What contractual/financial arrangements have been made? How are payments scheduled? Are progress checkpoints and

the approval process clearly delineated in the contract? Are progress payments tied to the approval process?

18. Are acceptance procedures clearly defined and agreed?

19. Are we in agreement on items such as warranties?

20. What reporting agreements have been made? Are they adequate? Is a communication plan in place?

21. Is this contractor financially stable? Is their management committed to this job?

22. Is proprietary information involved with this work? How will that be handled?

23. Do we have visibility for our work-in-progress? (I recall a client's representative being turned away from a subcontractor's workplace. They were told there were proprietary processes that could not be shared. The negotiations on that were interesting, to say the least. Guess what T's and C's were changed in all contracts from that client following that situation.)

Project Contracts Template

1. Does the PM and the team understand the contract? Do they have copies?

2. Has a Contract Administrator been assigned to the project?

3. Were contract changes made after the proposal submittal documented and relayed to the project team? (What you bid is seldom the same as what you win. Many changes are made during contract negotiations.)

4. Does the contract include a detailed plan for change control?

5. Is it clear to everyone who has the authority to make contractual commitments?

6. Did the organization's legal staff review and approve the T's and C's?

7. Is it clear who has the authority to make contractual commitments in the customer's shop?

8. Are all contracts reviewed by the legal staff— especially international agreements?

Abbreviations

BAU—Business as Usual

CCB—Change Control Board

COTS—Commercial-Off-the-Shelf

DeMo—Delivery Execution Model

EV—Earned Value

Earned Value terms:

>BCWS—Budgeted Cost of Work Scheduled

>BCWP—Budgeted Cost of Work Performed

>ACWP—Actual Cost of Work Performed

JIT—Just in Time

MIC—Management Information Center

PM—Project Manager

PMI—Project Management Institute. Provides guidelines for project management processes and procedures. Also one of the major certification bodies for Project Managers

PMR—Project Management Review

PDR—Preliminary Design Review

PRD—Project Requirements Document

PRINCE 2—European project management guidelines and certification

Procurement terms:

> RFI—Request for Information
>
> RFP—Request for Proposal
>
> RFQ—Request for Quote

RAM—Responsibility and Accountability Matrix

SLA—Service Level Agreement

SRR—Systems Requirement Review (Sometimes referred to as PRR—Project Requirements Review.)

SOW—Statement of Work

T's and C's —Contract Terms and Conditions

TIM—Technical Interchange Meeting

WBS—Work Breakdown Structure

About the Authors

Douglas Fain

Doug is a graduate of the Air Force Academy and has graduate degrees in Systems Management from the University of Southern California and Economics from Georgetown University. He spent 17 years with Martin Marietta working on aerospace programs such as the MX (Peacekeeper) project and the Magellan Mission to Venus. In 1993 he founded CEBG Consulting, an international business specializing in the management of large complex projects. Since then, he has consulted in many different industries across the globe, including projects such as major aircraft modifications, high-speed rail systems, laboratories, Ares I (shuttle replacement), cellular infrastructure, and Bureau of Reclamation pumping projects. He has consulted in 31 different countries for numerous corporations, four national governments, and the UN on over $30 Billion in projects around the world. In 1992 Doug was a candidate for the US Senate in Colorado and a surrogate speaker for the President of the United States. He has served on several boards and has over 30 years teaching experience in both graduate and undergraduate programs and has lectured in five universities. He has written three novels: an award winning novel *The Phantom's Song, 2040 American Exodus,* and *Anarchist for Rent.* Doug flew 214 combat missions in the F-4 Phantom fighter during the Vietnam War and earned a Distinguished Flying Cross for Heroism, a Distinguished Flying Cross for Achievement, 14 Air Medals, and an Air Force Commendation Medal.

Mark Hunt

Mark's early career in telecommunications engineering led him naturally into project management – that was 31 years ago! After reading an MBA in 1993, Mark founded Timeline Project Management to focus on delivering business and technical projects in some of the world's largest organizations. He quickly established a reputation for excellent leadership and project delivery skills, regardless of the type of project in question, and for his ability to quickly turn-around failing projects. For the last 25 years mark has worked in blue-chip and government organizations to deliver major projects in 14 countries. A chance over-dinner conversation with Doug, more than 20 years ago, peaked his interest in finding a better way to deliver projects, right-the-first-time - every time! Mark has appeared as a guest speaker in several global organizations and universities where he talks passionately about how good project management changes lives, and the economics of right-first-time project delivery.

39309231R00102

Made in the USA
Middletown, DE
18 March 2019